Hugo Assmann

PRACTICAL THEOLOGY OF LIBERATION

Hugo Assmann
PRACTICAL THEOLOGY OF LIBERATION
Teología desde la praxis de la liberación

Preface by Ernesto Cardenal

Introduction by Gustavo Gutiérrez

Translated from the Spanish by Paul Burns

Search Press London

First published in this translation
in Great Britain in 1975
by Search Press Limited
2-10 Jerdan Place LONDON SW6 5PT

Published originally by
Ediciones Sígueme, Salamanca
as TEOLOGIA DESDE LA PRAXIS DE LA LIBERACION: ENSAYO
TEOLOGICO DESDE LA AMERICA DEPENDIENTE, I.
Spanish original © Ediciones Sígueme 1973, 1975
This translation © Search Press Limited 1975
Translation of Introduction © Search Press Limited 1974, 1975
(from *Concilium* IV, 1974). Preface © Ernesto Cardenal & Search
Press 1975

ALL RIGHTS RESERVED NO PART OF THIS PUBLICATION MAY BE
STORED IN AN INFORMATION RETRIEVAL SYSTEM OR TRANSMITTED
OR REPRODUCED IN ANY FORM OR BY ANY MEANS KNOWN OR AS
YET UNKNOWN WHETHER ELECTRONIC MECHANICAL CHEMICAL
PHOTOCOPYING RECORDING MANUSCRIPT OR OTHERWISE FOR ANY
PURPOSE WHATSOEVER IN ANY COUNTRY WITHOUT THE PREVIOUS
WRITTEN PERMISSION OF SEARCH PRESS LIMITED 2-10 JERDAN PLACE
LONDON SW6 5PT GREAT BRITAIN

Printed and bound in Great Britain
by R. J. Acford Ltd, Chichester
ISBN: 0 85532 346 9

Contents

	Page
Preface	1
Introduction	5
Prefatory note	25
I The political dimension of faith: man's liberation in history	29
II Theology of liberation: a prospective evaluation	43
III Liberation: the implications of a new theological language	111
IV The Christian contribution to liberation in Latin America	129
Liberation: a protest song	146

Key to abbreviations

AID	International Development Association
ALALC	Latin American Free Trade Association
BID	Inter-American Development Bank
CECLA	Latin American Co-ordination Commission
CELAM	Latin American Episcopal Council
CEPAL	Latin American Economic Commission
CIA	Central Intelligence Agency
CIEC	Inter-American Catholic Education Conference
CNMC	National Morals and Civics Commission (Brazil)
ISAL	Church and Society in Latin America
MIEC	International Catholic Students Movement
MNR	National Revolutionary Movement (Bolivia)
OEA	Organization of American States

Preface: Revolution and theology

MEN cannot be sons of God if they are not fully men. Holiness cannot flourish in subhuman conditions. Therefore the first duty of the Christian now is to make the revolution. The revolutionary struggle is a priestly struggle, as Camilo Torres said.

The Church has a very important mission in these times in Latin America. I believe that its first responsibility is to preach communism. The greatest obstacle the revolution has in Latin America is a fear of "communism". Even the poor have this fear. I knew a very poor campesino in Nicaragua who feared communism because they were going to take away his chickens. The Church has contributed greatly to the inculcation of this fear in the people. Now the Church can be a very important factor in taking away the fear and thus speeding up the revolution. For that reason whenever I have an opportunity to preach to a large congregation (it is not always possible) I mention the word "communism".

Communism is deeply Christian. Moreover, it is the essence of Christianity. The word "communion" is the same as "communism". St Paul uses the same Greek word *koinonía* for the eucharistic communion and for the community of goods. And he uses the same word for the union of men with God which he calls the communion (or community of goods) of the Holy Spirit, or what we could call the communism that exists between God and men. Of course, for Paul, holding goods in common, the eucharist and the communion with the Holy Spirit are the same thing. When in the Epistle to the Hebrews he speaks of holding goods in common, he says that is the sacrifice which pleases God. As someone has said, it is the true Mass.

In Latin America, Christians and Marxists are joining forces to make the revolution and this is a new thing in the world. I believe that this will be the great contribution of Latin America to the world revolution. It deals with a Christianity different from what it was before – a Christianity that is not anti-revolutionary; and a different Marxism – one that is not anti-Christian.

Fidel Castro has said that a Christian can be revolutionary. And Che Guevara said that when Christians really become revolutionaries, the revolution in Latin America will be invincible. After this Latin American experience, neither Christianity nor Marxism is going to be the same as before.

In Venezuela I heard an old leader of the Communist Party say that now Christians were becoming revolutionary, the revolution would be possible in Latin America. They had believed before that the revolution could be achieved without Christians, but in that belief they had not been good Marxists because they had not taken into account that the people were Christian, and that a Christianless revolution would have to be a revolution without the people and hence a false revolution (we were at a big assembly of humble people most of whom were Christian and revolutionary).

And Fidel told me in Cuba that the contribution of the Christians is not only important to achieve the triumph of the revolution: it is even more important for what happens later: "for the sacrifices that the establishment of socialism demands".

If Marxists need Christians for the establishment of socialism, Christians need Marxists for the establishment of the kingdom of God on earth, so that the eucharist can be validly celebrated, as Camilo Torres said.

Garaudy, the French Communist, has dared to say that just as Christianity without Marxism would be incomplete, so would Marxism without St John of the Cross.

Another of the new contributions of Latin America is the theology of liberation. Theology of liberation is not one more chapter of traditional theology invented recently in Latin America, as European theologians are accustomed to believe. Just as there is a theology of marriage, a theology of the Church, a theology of the priesthood, a theology of work, and so on, they suppose the theology of liberation is one more appendix of traditional theology applied now to the theme of revolution. It is not so. This is an entirely new theology, one that replaces in the light of the revolution all the topics of traditional theology: God, Christ, the Church, the priesthood, marriage, work: everything, in fact.

This is a theology of the oppressed class, while the other is a theology of the dominant class. It is not practised by professional theologians for other professional theologians, as is the other. Instead it is usually the fruit of community reflection and is designed by men and women who belong to revolutionary communities. And it is for the use of these same communities. This theology is not usually carried on in books but in small magazines, simple leaflets, roneoed sheets. And as Giulio Girardi points out (precisely in one of those mimeographed papers) whereas one theology is purely intellectual, the other cannot be followed if one is not committed to the practice of revolution. One theology was helped by a philosophy (Aristotelianism). The other is helped by a science (Marxism). One theology was based on the Word of God (in the Bible). The other is based on the Bible but also on the Word of God as expressed in current events and in the newspapers: in other words, on political ground. As Giulio Girardi, one of the theologians of liberation, makes plain, our God is a living God who continues speaking in history. He didn't suddenly stop talking after the last book of the Bible.

This theology is based on the Bible but with a new interpretation of the Bible. That does not mean that we believe that the Bible can be interpreted as we please. But there is a revolutionary interpretation of the Scriptures just as there is a counter-revolutionary one. Jesus's words about turning the other cheek can be interpreted as not struggling against those who oppress the people. Here in my little commune in Solentiname in Nicaragua we comment every Sunday on the Gospel — the people and I. Once when that phrase of Jesus was being discussed a young campesino of our community,

Laureano, interpreted it like this: "It means that if the revolution has taken one piece of property from a rich man he should hand over the other property as well."

ERNESTO CARDENAL

Introduction: Liberation, theology and proclamation

THEOLOGY is an understanding of the faith and a re-reading of the word as it is lived in the Christian community. More than anything it has to do with the communication of faith and the proclamation of the good news, which is that the Father loves all men. To evangelize is to witness to that love; to say that it has been revealed to us and was made flesh in Christ.

The basis for talk about faith lies midway between experience and communication. Theology is concerned with our life as men and as Christians. It is a permanent yet ever-changing task. We have to *be* Christians within an historical process that is constantly transforming the conditions of human life. The Gospel has to be proclaimed to men who fulfil themselves in working out their own destiny. Theological discourse concerns a truth that is the way; it is about a word that is located in the midst of history. A task for all times, theology assumes different forms depending on the Christian experience and the preaching of the Gospel to men at a given moment of historical development.

Recent years in Latin America have been marked by a demanding discovery of another world: the poor, marginal and exploited class of society. In a social order which in terms of economics, politics and ideology was made by a few for their own benefit, the "others" (that is, the exploited lower classes, oppressed cultures and races subject to discrimination) are beginning to make their own voices heard. They are beginning to speak out directly and less and less through intermediaries; to rediscover themselves; and to make their unsettling presence felt in the system. They are increasingly less inclined to submit to demagogic manipulation and more or less disguised social assistance; instead they are gradually becoming the subjects of their own history and are forging a radically different society.

They can discover this only within the historical process of liberation, which seeks to build a truly egalitarian, fraternal and just society. For some time now, a growing number of Christians have been sharing in the process of liberation, and through it, in the discovery of the world of the exploited and peripheral people of the South American continent. This commitment gives rise to a new way of being a man and a believer, of living and thinking the faith, of being called together in an "ecclesia" or church.

This sharing of Christians in the process of liberation varies in radicalism and is virtually a process of searching and advancing by "trial and error". At times it gets bogged down at difficult points in the road; at times it moves at great speed. But it follows a path whose new significance for theological reflection and for the communal celebration of faith is gradually becoming clear.

I only want to make a few observations about a theological task which begins from the historical practice, or "praxis", of liberation, through which the poor and oppressed of this world are endeavouring to build a different social order and a new way of being men. This theological reflection is impelled by a desire to speak the word of the Lord to all men from that position of solidarity.

1. *The practice of liberation*

The irruption of the other, the poor man, into our lives leads to active solidarity with his interests and his struggles. This commitment is expressed in an attempt to transform a social order which breeds marginalization and oppression. Participation in the historical practice of liberation is ultimately the practice of love, the love of Christ in one's neighbour; and of encounter with the Lord in the midst of a history ridden with conflicts.

2. Who has been this man's neighbour?

Rediscovering our neighbour means entering his world. It also means a break with ours. The world of inward-looking absorption with self, the world of the "old man" socio-culturally conditioned. To enter the world of the other, the poor man, and its demands, is to begin to be a "new man". It is a process of conversion.

Love for my neighbour is an essential component of the Christian life. But if I think of my neighbour as the man "near me", the one I meet on *my* way, the one who comes *to me* seeking aid ("Who is *my* neighbour?"), my world remains the same. All individual gestures of aid, all superficial reform of society is a love that stays comfortably at home ("If they love those who love them, what reward will they have?"). If, on the other hand, I consider my neighbour as the man in *whose* path I deliberately place myself, the man "distant" from me, the one whom I approach ("Which of these three was neighbour *to this man*?"); if I make myself the neighbour of the man I seek out in streets and squares, in factories and marginal *barrios*, in the fields and the mines, my world changes. That is what happens when an authentic and effective "option for the poor" is made; because, for the Gospel, a poor man is the neighbour *par excellence*. On this option turns a new way of being a man and being a Christian in Latin America.

But the "poor" do not exist as an act of destiny; their existence is not politically neutral or ethically innocent. The poor are a by-product of the system in which we live and for which we are responsible. The poor are marginalized in our social and cultural world. They are the oppressed, the exploited, the workers cheated of the fruits of their work, and stripped of their being as men. The poverty of the poor is not an appeal for generous action to relieve it, but a demand for the construction of a different social order.

It is, however, necessary to take one more step. The option for the poor and the oppressed through a liberating commitment leads to a realization that this commitment cannot be isolated from the social set-up to which they belong; otherwise we would not go beyond "being sorry for the situation".

The poor, the oppressed, are members of a culture which is not respected, a race which is discriminated against, a social class subtly or openly exploited by another social class. To opt for the poor is to opt for the marginalized and exploited, to take stock of the social conflict and to side with the dispossessed. To opt for the poor is to enter the world of the oppressed race or culture or social class; to enter the universe of their values and cultural categories. That means solidarity with their interests and their struggles.

The poor man is someone who questions the ruling social order. Solidarity with the poor means realizing the injustice on which that order is built, and the countless means it employs to maintain itself. It also means understanding that we cannot be *for* the poor and oppressed if we are not *against* all that gives rise to man's exploitation of man. For this same reason, solidarity is more than just saying No to the way things are. It must be an effort to forge a society in which the worker is not subordinated to the owner of the means of production; a society in which the assumption of social responsibility for political affairs will include social responsibility for real liberty, and will lead to the emergence of a new social consciousness.

Solidarity with the poor implies the transformation of the existing social order. It implies a liberating social praxis: that is, a transforming activity directed towards the creation of a free and just society.

3. History and liberating love

During the last two centuries man has begun to realize his capacity to transform the world in which he lives, and to do it swiftly and in a controlled manner. That experience has changed the course of history and given a definitive character to our age. Unsuspected possibilities have opened up for man's life on earth, but their appropriation for the benefit of a minority of the human race has provoked the frustration and exasperation of the dispossessed masses.

The industrial revolution, as it was called, meant the beginning of a stage of broad and rapid production of consumer goods for man, based on a hitherto unknown capacity to transform nature.[1] The use of experimental science had already set in motion the attempt to dominate nature, but this mastery was only to reach full consciousness and maturity when scientific knowledge was translated into ways of manipulating the material world, and into the possibility of satisfying the vital needs of man on a large scale.[2] The productive powers of man increased beyond predictable limits and brought about a revolutionary change in the economic activity of society. The process has continued, and advances spirally. Today we are in the middle of what is called a second industrial revolution. All this has led man to feel that he is capable of modifying his living conditions radically, and has given a clear and stimulating affirmation of his freedom vis-à-vis Nature. It has also produced the widest-ranging differences among the peoples of the earth that history has ever known.

One of the most uncontrolled consequences of the industrial revolution was the progressive displacement of man by the machine. This created a marginal social surplus in the course of the production of wealth: the so-called "reserve industrial pool" consisting of a growing mass of marginalized people not reabsorbed by the system. The nineteenth century was slow to take account of this social price for the accelerated rhythm of industrialization and the corresponding technological boom. Furthermore, as technical progress became more and more refined, and the standard of living of the developed countries rose, the process was accompanied by an international division of labour which produced vast differences between one country and another.

Even though the industrial revolution has given modern man a unique situation and power to transform nature, it has intensified social contradictions until an international crisis situation has been reached which forceful measures can no longer hide.

These consequences of the industrial revolution make for a better understanding of another historical process, whose origins go back to the same period and reveal another aspect of man's transforming action. I refer to the political field, which experienced in the French Revolution the practical possibility of a profound transformation of the existing social order. It declared the right of every man to share in the running of the society to which he belongs. With all its ambiguities, that event put an end to one kind of society; from then on the people as a whole aspired to an effective share in political power and an active part in history: in short, they wanted a truly democratic society. Again we are faced with a new affirmation of man's freedom, this time in relation to social organization. But for a truly democratic organization of society there must be just economic conditions; if these do not exist in underdeveloped countries, or in their external relations with developed countries, explosive tensions occur — in national and international contexts.

Philosophers living at the start of the Revolutionary era were acutely conscious of being on the threshold of a new historical era marked by critical reason and man's transforming liberty.[3] All that would lead, they thought, to a different man, more master of himself, and of his destiny in history. History could no longer be thought of in terms of a nature divorced from society. The industrial revolution and the political revolution were to appear with increasing clarity not as two processes which happened to be contemporary or convergent, but as two inter-dependent movements. As they advanced, their reciprocal involvement became more evident. To transform history requires a simultaneous transformation in nature and society. In this transforming praxis, there is more than a new consciousness of the meaning of economic and political action — there is a new way of being man in history.

To see a transformation of history from the standpoint of dominated countries and marginalized men, the poor of this world, leads us to see it as liberating action. That means seeing in it something which is perhaps missed when it is viewed from the standpoint of the minority of the human race who control most scientific and technical assets and political power in the world today. That is why a liberating praxis has a subversive look about it: that is only natural, in a social order where people are only just beginning to listen to the poor, the "others".[4]

What is really at stake is not a greater rationalization of economic activity or a better social organization, but through them the whole question of justice and love. The terms are traditional and perhaps hardly current in strictly political language, but they recall the human reality at the heart of the matter. They remind us that we are speaking of men, of whole peoples who are suffering poverty and exploitation, who cannot exercise the most elementary human rights, and who scarcely know they are men. That is why a liberating praxis, in so far as it starts from authentic solidarity with the poor and the oppressed, is specifically a practice of love: effective historical love for men of flesh and blood. Then love of our neighbour is love of Christ, who is identified with the very least of our brothers. Any attempt to separate the love of God from the love of our neighbour gives rise to attitudes which impoverish the one or the other. It is easy to set a "heavenly practice" against an "earthly practice", and *vice versa*: easy, but not in accord with the Gospel of God made man. It is genuine and more profound to speak of a practice of love which is rooted in the gratuitous love of the Father, and which makes itself history in solidarity with the poor and dispossessed, and through them in solidarity with all men.

4. Believing and understanding

Commitment to the process of liberation, with all its political demands, means tackling the world of the poor and the oppressed in an effective way. That puts a new spiritual requirement at the very heart of liberation: the matrix of a new theological reflection, of an apprehension of the Word, the free gift of God, breaking into human existence and transforming it.

The practice of liberation must lead one to become poor with the poor. For the committed Christian, it is a way of identifying with Christ, who came into the world to preach the Gospel to the poor and liberate the oppressed. Evangelical poverty was and is to be lived as an act of liberation and love towards the poor of this world, as solidarity with them and as protest against the poverty in which they lived and live; as identification with the interests of the oppressed classes and a rejection of the exploitation of which they were and are the victims. If the ultimate cause of the exploitation and alienation of man is egotism, the underlying motive of voluntary poverty is love for one's neighbour. Poverty — the result of social injustice, which has its deepest roots in sin — is accepted not to make it an ideal of life but to witness the evil it represents. The condition of the sinner, and its consequences, were accepted by Christ, not to idealize them, but out of love and solidarity with men, and to redeem them from sin; to fight against human egotism and abolish all injustice and division among men. Consequently, poverty lived in true imitation of Christ, instead of separating us from the world, places us at the very heart of the situation of exploitation and oppression, and from there proclaims liberation and full communion with the Lord. Spiritual poverty is preached and lived as a way of being totally at God's disposal; as a spiritual childhood.[5]

All this means entering a different world and outlines a Christian experience as yet untried, full of possibilities and promise, but with no lack of sharp turns and blind alleys on the route ahead. There is no smooth triumphant highway for the life of faith. Absorption in the political demands of a liberating commitment can lead to difficulties. The tensions of living in solidarity with exploited people who belong to a Church containing many members on the side of the prevailing social order, can cause some to lose the dynamism of their faith and suffer the anguish of a dichotomy between their Christian existence and their political action. And there are those who see their love for God vanish in favour of a love which he himself has inspired and nourished; the love of man, a love which, unable to observe the unity demanded by the Gospel, remains heedless of the plenitude God contains in himself.

Such cases exist. To be present in the frontier areas of the Christian community, where the revolutionary commitment is at its most intense, is not a tranquil experience. The clues to any solution can only arise from the depths of the problem itself. Protective measures conceal reality and delay a useful response. They neglect the urgency and gravity of the reasons which lead to a commitment to men exploited by a cruel, impersonal system; and they show a lack of belief in the strength of the Gospel and of faith.

For many Christians a liberating commitment now means an authentic *spiritual experience*, in the original biblical sense of the term; a living in the Spirit which makes us recognize ourselves as free and creative sons of the Father and brothers of man ("God has sent into our hearts the Spirit of the Son who proclaims Abba, Father"). In Christ we become simultaneously and inseparably sons and brothers ("Whoever sees me sees the Father; whoever does the will of my Father, he is my brother"). Only through acts of love and solidarity will our encounter be effective with the poor, with the exploited man, and in him our encounter with Christ (". . . you gave it to me"). Our denial of love and solidarity will be a rejection of Christ (" . . . you refused it to me"). The poor man, the other, reveals the totally Other to us. That is what is involved: life in the presence of the Lord, at the centre of an activity in one way or another related to the political world, with its confrontation of interests and conflicts and the need for a degree of scientific rationality to understand it in its complexity. We need "contemplatives in political action". We are unused to this. A spiritual experience seems to us something to be found a long way from human realities as impure as political action. The form of our entry into the realities of politics will depend on our situation in society and in the church community. However, that is where we are going, towards an encounter with the Lord not in the poor man "isolated and good", but in the oppressed man, fighting ardently for his most elementary rights and for the construction of a society in which men can live as men. History is the scene of the revelation God makes of the mystery of his person. His word reaches us insofar as we are involved in the evolution of history.

To opt for the poor man, to be identified with his lot, to share his destiny, means a desire to turn history into genuine brotherhood for all men. It means accepting the free gift of sonship and opting for the cross of Christ in the hope and joy of his Resurrection.

In these concrete conditions comes the process of conversion, the nodal point of all spirituality. Conversion means going out of oneself, being open to God and others; it implies a break, but above all it means following a new path. For that very reason, it is not an inward-looking, private attitude, but a process which occurs in the socio-economic, political and cultural medium in which life goes on, and which is to be transformed. The encounter with Christ in the poor man constitutes an authentic spiritual experience. It is a living in the Spirit, the bond of love between Father and Son, God and man, man and man. Christians committed to an historical praxis of liberation try to live this kind of profound communion. They find the love of Christ in their encounter with the poor and in solidarity with them: they find faith in our situation as sons of the Father working for a society of brothers: and they find hope in the salvation of Christ, in commitment to the liberation of the oppressed.

This is a unifying experience which all too often seems impoverished by any attempt to express it. That may be due to its handling by theologians who tend to separate and even set at odds the elements of the essential experience; or it may be due to the defensive attitude adopted against Christians who see in the commitment to liberation a challenge to their privileges in the present social order. The Christian experience involved is not without risk of simplistic identifications and reductions; but it is a bold and profound attempt to live in Christ by taking on oneself the history of suffering and injustice of the poor of this continent. To the extent that this experience has achieved genuine expression, it has already offered rich possibilities for the whole Church.

5. *Understanding faith*

The act of faith is at the root of all theology. It is not there as mere intellectual acceptance of the message, but as a warm welcome for the gist of the Word heard in the community of the Church; as an encounter with the Lord; as love for our brother. Faith has to do with Christian existence as a whole. To welcome the Word, to make it life, we need action: a starting-point for apprehending faith. That is the meaning of St Anselm's *"Credo ut intelligam"*: "I do not try, Lord, to penetrate your depths, because my intelligence could not manage that; but I want to some extent to understand your truth, which my heart believes and loves. I do not seek to understand so as to believe; but *I believe in order to understand*, since I am sure that if I did not believe, I would not understand".

The primacy of God and the grace of faith give theological work its *raison d'être*. If we begin there we can see that, in the end, a Christian cannot understand his faith as part of the "imitation of Christ", which means thinking, feeling and acting like Jesus. An authentic theology is always a spiritual theology; that was how the Fathers understood it. The life of faith is not only the point of departure but the point of arrival for the task which theology sets itself. Belief and understanding are part of a circle.

Theology always employs a certain rationale, even if it does not identify with it. This rationale corresponds to the cultural universe of the believer. Every theology asks itself about the meaning of the Word of God for us in history now, and attempts at a reply are made in terms of our culture and the problems which face men of our time. From the standpoint of this cultural universe we reshape the message of the Gospel and the faith for our contemporaries and ourselves.

That is what Thomistic theology, for example, attempted, using Aristotelian philosophy and the whole world vision to which it was tied. That was a step of first importance in the understanding of faith. Today we are witnessing a crisis of the traditional rationale in theology. Among the results is the philosophical eclecticism of a certain contemporary philosophy. Another result is the efforts which we see, not so much to rebuild an impossible unitary theological system, as rather to find new ways of formulating the Word. In a more radical manner, perhaps, this has provoked questioning in cognition theory, or the theory of knowledge: an area not perhaps given sufficient attention in theology. On what assumptions does theology base its approach to historical reality? What is the influence on our theological reflection of the place held by the institutional Church in present-day society? Where does the theologian speak from? For what and for whom does he speak? What is theology as a practical task?

An important role in these queries is played by scientific knowledge, especially when history or psychology is touched upon. The sciences are forms of expression of human reason; they reveal to us aspects of nature and man which evade other approaches to these realities; they must not be neglected by theology. Philosophical reflection, even when opening up new paths, preserves all its validity and is enriched in permanent dialogue with the sciences. It also answers questions which do not belong to the domain of the sciences; and it makes its own contribution to the knowledge of history and to the role of the free, creative action of man. This complexity and wide-ranging character of human knowledge is set to work in the historical practice of liberation, and makes it more effective. It is also present in any discourse on faith from a position of solidarity with the poor and oppressed.

Much contemporary theology seems to start from the challenge of the non-believer. He questions our religious world and faces it with a demand for purification and renewal. Bonhoeffer took up the challenge and put the incisive question which is at the root of many theological endeavours nowadays: How is God to be proclaimed in an adult world? This challenge in a continent like Latin America does not come primarily from the non-believer, but from the *man who is not a man*, who is not recognized as such by the existing social order: he is in the ranks of the poor, the exploited; he is the man who is systematically and legally despoiled of his being as a man: who scarcely knows that he *is* a man. His challenge is not aimed first at our religious world, but at our *economic, social, political and cultural world*; therefore it is an appeal for the revolutionary transformation of the very bases of a dehumanizing society. *The question therefore is not how to speak of God in an adult world, but how to proclaim him as a Father in a world that is not human.* What is implied in telling this man who is not a man that he is a son of God? To some extent these were the questions put by Bartolomé de las Casas and many others in the sixteenth century on the basis of their encounter with the American natives. The discovery of the other, of the exploited, led to reflection about the demands of faith opposite to that of those who sided with the rulers.

Today the historical framework is different and the social analysis has changed, but we are witnessing the rediscovery of the poor man in Latin America. Solidarity with him means deliberate entry into the arena of history, into confrontation between countries and between social classes. It means entry on the side of the dominated and oppressed. However, the social system itself, which creates and justifies that situation of oppression, is not really questioned unless a part is played in the efforts to transform it radically and forge a different order. Practising liberation means facing the complexity and variety of human knowledge; ultimately it means entering a different cultural world.

From within this cultural world in which we are situated due to our involvement in the Latin American historical process, we try to reformulate the Gospel message. From this viewpoint discourse on faith follows a different path from that taken when the challenge of the non-believer is the starting-point. Theology will be a critical reflection from and about the historical praxis of liberation in confrontation with the Word of the Lord lived and accepted in faith. It will be a reflection in and about faith as a liberating practice: an understanding of faith on the basis of a choice; thought arising from a commitment to create a just, fraternal society; and a duty to help make that commitment fuller and more radical. Theological discourse becomes truth (is verified) on insertion into the process of liberation.

To reflect on the faith as liberating practice is to reflect on a truth which is made, and not just affirmed;[6] it is to start from a promise which is fulfilled throughout history and at the same time opens history beyond itself. In the final instance the exegesis of the Word, to which theology tries to contribute, is accomplished in deeds. This factor, not mere affirmation, will rescue the understanding of faith from idealism.

6. *Evangelization and "Ecclesia"*

Entry into the process of liberation is a profound and decisive spiritual experience at the very heart of an historical commitment, with necessary political implications.

We are not faced with new applications of old theological notions, but with a need to live and think the faith in different socio-cultural categories. In this search, urgency demands that the Word of the Lord should be proclaimed in our everyday language.

That is the point at issue; a re-reading of the Gospel message from the standpoint of liberating practice. Theological discourse mediates between a new way of living the faith, and its communication. If theology is a re-reading of the Gospel, then it is expressed here in terms of the proclamation of the message.

To know that the Lord loves us and to welcome the free gift of his love is a profound source of joy for the man who lives by his Word. To communicate that joy is to evangelize: it means communicating the good news of the love of God, which has changed our lives, and communicating it freely, just as the love which originated it was given freely. The task of evangelization always starts from an experience of the Lord: a living of the love of the Father, who makes us sons and transforms us by making us more fully men and brothers of men.

To proclaim the Gospel is to proclaim the mystery of sonship and brotherhood, a mystery hidden from all ages and now revealed in Christ. To proclaim the Gospel therefore is to call people together in an "ecclesia", to unite them in an assembly. It is only in a community that faith can be lived in love; only there can it be celebrated and deepened; only there can it be lived in one gesture: as fidelity to the Lord and solidarity with all men. To accept the Word is to convert the Other into others, the rest. We live this Word with them. Faith cannot be lived on a private, inward-looking plane because faith rejects all turning in upon oneself. In the dynamism of the good news which reveals us as sons of the Father and brothers one of another, we experience the creation of a community, of the Church, which will be a visible sign to men of their liberation in Christ. This proclamation of the Gospel calling us together in an "ecclesia" is made from a choice of active solidarity with the interests and struggles of the poor, of the exploited classes. That means a real break with the way of living, thinking and communicating the faith in the Church today. That demands a conversion to another world, a new style of understanding the faith, and a reformulation of the message.[7]

In this reformation, what has come to be called the political dimension of the Gospel takes on a new face. It is now obvious that there is no question of adding something from outside the Gospel by yielding to partisan pressures of our age, but that we are in the presence of an offshoot of the Gospel. Moreover, the political dimension is accepted frankly and openly. Its precise extent has still to be defined, and any simplistic view of it must be avoided, but our political conviction grows even firmer. The gift of sonship is lived in history. By making men brothers, we welcome this gift, not in words but in deeds ("Not all who say to me Lord, Lord, will enter the Kingdom of Heaven, but he who does the will of my Father"). To struggle against all injustice and exploitation, to be committed to the creation of a more brotherly and human society, is to live the love of the Father, and to bear witness to it.

The proclamation of a God who loves all men equally must be given substance in history and must become history. To proclaim that love in a profoundly unequal society marked by injustice and the exploitation of some groups by others, of one social class by another social class, will make this process of "becoming history" a conflict-laden experience. Hence the political dimension lies within the dynamism of a Word seeking to become incarnate in history. The demands of the Gospel are incompatible with the social situation which is being lived in Latin America, with the ways in which relations between men operate, with the structures in which these relations are found. More is required than the rejection of some individual injustice or other; we are faced with the need for a different social order. Only a certain degree of political maturity will permit a true political understanding of the Gospel and will prevent it from being reduced to an aid programme, however sophisticated, or to a simple task of "human promotion". It will also avoid the reduction of the evangelizing task to a form of political action with its own laws and demands.

Authentic proclamation of the love of God, of brotherhood and of the radical equality of all men, to the exploited man of our continent, will show him that his situation is opposed to the Gospel; and that will help him to appraise the profound injustice of such a state of affairs. The oppressed sectors will acquire a clear political consciousness only by direct participation in the struggles of the people. Nevertheless, in the complex totality of the political process which must break with an oppressive social order and lead to a brotherly society, the ideological struggle has an important place. In Latin America, the whole Christian set-up is made to play an important part inside the dominant ideology, which helps to strengthen and affirm a society divided into antagonistic classes. Conservative sectors in fact frequently appeal to Christian ideas to justify the social order which serves their interests and maintains their privileges. That is why the communication of the message re-read from the standpoint of the other, of the poor and oppressed, will serve to unmask any attempt to ideologize the Gospel and justify a situation contrary to the most elemental demands of the Word.

7. *Liberating evangelization*

Are we faced with a political reduction of the Gospel? Escaping from one ideological use of Christianity, are we falling into another? The danger exists; it would be ingenuous or dishonest to deny it. We have to remember that re-reading the Gospel from the standpoint of solidarity with the poor and the oppressed enables us to condemn the way those in power fetter the Gospel in order to place it at the service of their own interests. We cannot do that properly, if we are not aware of the permanently creative and critical nature of the liberating message of the Gospel. This message is not identified with any social form, however just it may appear to us at the time. The word of the Lord places every historical achievement within the broad perspective of the radical and total liberation of Christ, the Lord of history. A reversion to an ideology made to justify a particular social situation is inevitable when the Gospel is not lived as the word of a Father who loves us freely and gratuitously, with a love which renews the face of the earth, and calls us always to a new life in his Son.

The liberation that comes from Christ is not to be reduced to a religious plane tangential to the concrete world of men, as those who wish to domesticate the gospel claim. The salvation of Christ is in fact so full that nothing escapes it. Evangelization is liberating because it is a message of total freedom, which necessarily includes a demand for the transformation of the historical and political conditions in which men live. But that liberation leads this same history beyond itself, to a fullness beyond the reach of anything that can be done or foreseen by human beings. The men who are the objects of the Gospel message are not abstract, a-political beings, but members of a society marked by injustice and the exploitation of some men by others. Similarly, the Christian community from which the message is proclaimed and which most of these men belong to in one way or another, is no reality outside history. Its past and present link it closely to the history of the Latin American people from early on. Without an historical perspective, it is not possible to grasp what is involved in evangelizing a people to whom the Gospel has already been proclaimed, and when it is a part of their lives in one way or another. On the other hand, we have to take into account the situation of a Church which for the most part is tied to the actual social order of Latin America, if we are to grasp what is implied by the liberating character of that evangelization.

8. *Solidarity with the poor and the people of God*

The proclamation of the Gospel from the standpoint of identification with the poor calls the Church to solidarity with the lower classes of the continent; to solidarity with their aspirations and with their struggle to take a part in Latin American history. The Church is called to make a contribution from its own task, the proclamation of the Gospel, to the abolition of a society built by and for the benefit of a few, and to the construction of a different social order, more just and more human, for all men and women.

This process leads to profound breaks and re-orientations in the Church of today. They will not, however, be fertile if they express only a personal anguish, and identity crisis, emotional reactions or impatience, however legitimate all these may be. That leads only to defensive attitudes, authoritarian measures, gestures inspired by fear or by a search for security, and an endless spiral of conflicts inside the Church. Breaks and reorientations must be radical; they have to go to the very root of the matter, which in this case extends beyond a narrowly ecclesiastical area. That root is the way to be a man and a Christian in the present reality of Latin America; that way consists of identification with the oppressed classes of a continent of injustice and exploitation, which is also a continent of thirst for liberation and hope.

This is to assume that new experiments are being made in evangelization and in convocation into an "ecclesia".[8] There will be different ways of being present in the world of the people, quite beyond any institutional rigidity. We must be prepared to listen to a different voice from the one we are accustomed to hear in the Church. We must inculcate critical awareness of the social and cultural categories which bind fast our way of living and proclaiming the Gospel, making it alien to the world of dominated peoples, races and classes, and even contrary to their profound aspirations towards liberation. And of course we must also take for granted an authentic search for the Lord in this encounter with the poor, and a lucid explanation of what that spiritual experience signifies.

We envisage the creation of Christian communities in which the private owners of the goods of this world cease to be the masters of the Gospel; communities in which the dispossessed can bring about a social approximation of the Gospel. Such groups will be prophetic and proclaim a Church wholly at the service of men in their battle to be men, one that will always be creative and critical, because rooted in the Gospel. This struggle for manhood follows a way difficult to understand from the old world in which the Word has been and still is lived, thought and proclaimed. Only by putting down roots among alienated, exploited men and by rising from among these men themselves, from their aspirations, interests, struggles and cultural categories, will a people of God be forged which will be a Church of the people; one which will bring *all* men to listen to the gospel message; one which will be a sign of the liberation of the Lord of history.

None of this would have meaning or could even be glimpsed if it were not already sketchily apparent in trials now being made in various parts of the continent. These attempts start off from the entry of a growing number of Christian groups — workers, professional men, peasants, students, bishops, priests — into the process of liberation in Latin America. Their entry is official and unofficial. It needs greater profundity, experience, clarity and purification. It will have to function critically within any too simplistic political process which fails to take into account all the dimensions of man. It will have to grow so that the voice of the Christian people of the lower classes is heard in their own language. There are difficulties. The terrain offers hard going at times, with hostility and resistance from those, whether Christians or not, who are tied to the old order of things. But the fruits of liberation, understanding of the faith, and proclamation of the Gospel are already apparent.

Present times in Latin America do not allow for euphoria. The spirituality of exodus is no less important than that of exile. Before the joy of resurrection comes death on the cross — and that can take various forms. But hope is always there. The situation which we are living through in Latin America will, we hope, enable us to experience and understand in a new form what Paul called "hoping against all hope".

GUSTAVO GUTIÉRREZ

NOTES

1 Cf. Eric Hobsbawm's classic work, *The Age of Revolution: Europe 1789-1848* (London, 1962).
2 In its early stages the industrial revolution received some impetus from the inventive work of artisans. Shortly after that it made dynamic progress following scientific advances.
3 Cf. Kant, *Philosophy of History* and Hegel, *Lessons on the Philosophy of History*. See Ernst Cassirer, *The Philosophy of the Enlightenment* (New York & London, 1959).
4 For the political options now being taken in Latin America in this regard see my *Theology of Liberation* (New York, 1973; London, 1974), chapters 6 and 7.
5 *Theology of Liberation, op. cit.*, ch. 13.
6 Note in this perspective the reflections of Duns Scotus on theology as a practical science.
7 "The biblical hermeneutic will differ according as we consider the

God of the Bible as totally distinct, with nothing in common with the universe in which man is so profoundly integrated, or simply as the Other 'whose ways are not our ways (Is. 55. 8), nor his thoughts our thoughts, but yet 'We are indeed his offspring' (Acts 17. 28)." Cazelles, *Ecriture, Parole et Esprit* (Paris, 1970), p. 76.
8 Cf. Karl Rahner on a Church of the future in *The Shape of the Church to Come* (London & New York, 1974).

Prefatory note

I CAN think of nothing more challenging to a Christian and a theologian than these verses written by a companion of mine deeply committed to the liberation of his fellow men. He is just one of many people who no longer believe what Christians believe, yet one who would like to think that they are right.

When you succeed in changing
all your abstract nouns
for a few concrete ones
whose meaning can be felt,
perhaps it will make sense again
for you to talk to us of Christ and God.
When it is seen to be true,
in a way that can be genuinely proclaimed,
that Justice has "pitched its tent in our midst",
and that Love has "dwelt amongst us",
then perhaps what your Bible calls
the "name of God"
can make itself known.

This book aims to be the word of action rather than the action of the word. It tells of our situation as oppressed peoples. It sees faith as the historical process of liberation. Essentially, it is about a "great event" — taking the first step. It is about those who take a risk, and about the risks they take. Of course actions speak louder than words, and the words in this book, although they concern action, are not action itself. They can only allude to it. That is the only dignity they have. If what they refer to doesn't exist, they have no dignity at all — for author or for reader.

HUGO ASSMANN

I The political dimension of faith:
man's liberation in history

I The political dimension of faith: man's liberation in history

THIS chapter is a quest for an appropriate context. If it seems tight or condensed, that is because I am trying to set out the basic concepts and therefore terms needed to think in an intellectually responsible way about the historico-political dimension of Christian commitment. I don't intend to give an academic account of the various schools of European political theology. I am more concerned with the actual Latin American context.[1]

1. The traditional meaning of political theology

It starts as a "theological" justification for "reasons of state"; the clear ideological aim is to legitimize the *status quo*. There are many varieties of this kind of political theology throughout history, and even some "Christian" ones.

Classic examples are the *politike* theology of the ancient Greeks; the *civilis* theology of the Romans; the political theologies of "Christendom" (de Bonald, de Maistre, Donoso Cortès, and so on).

A contemporary example is the place of religion in the "Moral and Civic Education" programme in Brazil: "Religion, morals and civics may be seen ideally as three concentric circles, with religion as the outer, morals the middle and civics the inner. Then civil duties, rights and actions form part of a wider grouping of moral duties, rights and actions, and morality is tied to permanent principles coming from God" (CNMC, doc. 1 3, 2).

Any type of "Christendom", whether right- or left-wing, features a legitimating political theology of this kind, whose essence is the epiphany, or manifestation, of God in its institutions.

2. The new European political theology

The principal exponents of this political theology are J. B. Metz and Jürgen Moltmann. Conscious of the historical burden of the term "political theology", they are determined to avoid new forms of theological support for the existing power structures. They are trying instead to do away with the theologies that justify the *status quo*. And those theologies are still operative in present-day Christianity.

A new link between theology and politics is now possible precisely because our understanding of politics has changed.

(*a*) The distinction between state and society means that political activity can no longer be reduced to the citizen-state relationship (powers established by the electorate). The realm of politics is everything embraced by the term "society", and not only formal relationships with the state. Everything in society has a political dimension.

(*b*) If nominal democracies narrow the sphere of politics to the periodic casting of a vote, they continue the social dualism. They remove one area belonging to the realm of "politics" from the other, "ordinary" area of daily non-political affairs, and thus contradict their basic democratic requirement — which is that the overall political order should be an "order of freedom": that is, a constant creative process of reformation by all those citizens who participate at any level of decision-making. In such a state of contradiction, however, democratic ideals are turned into an ideology whose working obscures the true rules of the game.

From a theological point of view, the new political theology aims at:

(*a*) being a *critical corrective* to any relegation of faith to the private sphere — a tendency apparent even in progressive circles. The transcendental, existentialist and personalist schools of theology tend in this direction. Bultmann's "existential hermeneutics" is fundamentally a-political. As Metz has pointed out, much Catholic post-Vatican II language is infected in this way; the effect is the promotion of a dual standard in human life: "Love, like all interhuman phenomena, is emphatically stressed, but is seen, from the start and almost self-evidently, as valuable only in its private and depoliticized form: as an I-you relationship, an interpersonal or local community relationship. The dominant category is that of personal encounter.";

(*b*) emphasizing the *political dimension of faith*, by introducing its basic tenets (grace, redemption, salvation, sin, and so on) into the fullness of the historical process;

(*c*) reflecting in new terms on the relationship between *theory* and *practice*;

(*d*) regarding the Church as an *institution of social criticism*, an institution of the critical freedom of faith;

(*e*) redeeming the *dangerous memory*, the subversive contents, the cries of frustrated hope (Metz) in the history of Christianity and in the Christian message.

Because it unleashed an enormous storm-wave of discussion, and because of the very vagueness of its statements, European political theology was forced, in its second stage, to offer a great number of theoretical clarifications and sub-distinctions. When confronted with unashamedly reactionary elements, it ingenuously accepted their rules of the game, thereby losing something of its initial emotive power. Furthermore, its actual social analysis remained deplorably vague, even with regard to the affluent world from which it sprang, not to speak of the needs of the Third World.[3] Nevertheless, its basic intuitions remain extremely important.

In any case, the debate goes on. It arouses definite hopes, despite Metz's basic error in returning to the distinction between political ethics and political theology, and thereby distancing himself from the practical context. Another error of the European theologians is to take too little notice of Marx in their reworking of the relationship between theory and practice.

3. What is political action?

The narrow view of politics as "party politics" has to be superseded, if not dispensed with, if we are to arrive at a definition of political action.

Without denying — but, on the contrary, stressing — the importance of personal development, and so of inter-personal and small-group relationships, all gaps between this private world and what happens in the broader context of society as a whole must be filled. Politicizing private life doesn't mean threatening its precious inner core of personal intensity, but making it conscious of its true historical character.

Nominally a-political stances, such as the Church taking refuge in its "spiritual mission" as an excuse for opting out of the political arena, can usually be identified with a specific political viewpoint. Carried to an extreme, a-politicism leaves the world free for the "principalities and powers" of social demonology to continue without interference, and therefore has an important political function. Dualisms are the ideological roots of reaction.

Every political ethic based on "law and order" tends to narrow the operational field of politics, for it de-politicizes one area of human activity. Every political ethic based on "change", on the other hand, tends to extend and universalize political consciousness and action.

Hence the expansion or contraction of the idea of political action itself is tied to the prevalence of change, or the maintenance of the established order. Of course it is possible for the "de-politicized" to be "politically" mobilized by the ploys of self-interested defenders of the *status quo*, while in fact they are being made to abdicate any real political responsibility. This might be called "de-politicized political action".

Every human act, even the most private, possesses not only a social content (because it transcends the individual), but a political content (because that transcending of the individual is always related to change *or* stability in society).

Political consciousness means awareness of the basic fact that all human actions have a political dimension, and of the implications of this fact in the light of man's ethical responsibilities, in a particular situation at a certain time and place in history.

Political action means acting in accordance with the responsibilities revealed by political consciousness, which takes account of the particular implications of the essential political dimension of all human acts. In other words, political action is an effective acceptance of the historical character of human existence.

The implications for political theology are these: a theology of the historico-political development of man is only possible (and basically necessary) in so far as it relates to an ethic of change, and in so far as it accepts political action as a means of transforming society. Such a political theology has to desacralize not only nature, but all the institutions of the *status quo*. It also has to put the new institutions brought about by change in a human perspective. It must never accept the ethics of the "establishment". Even when the revolution is victorious, that theology will tend to remain as a revolutionary force. Once it accepts an established order, a political theology will necessarily revert to the legitimizing function of political theology in the classical sense.

4. *The new primacy of politics*

The primacy of politics shows our realization that all other dimensions of human activity (technology, science and even individuality) require a broader "why" — or meaning. No partisan ethics, such as a professional morality, can be sufficient in itself; a wider ethics is necessary if the question "why?" is to have any depth. Instead of looking for an answer outside history, men have learnt to seek it in history. This confrontation with its historical character has shown them the primacy of politics.

Social revolutions have been the basic means of bringing about this realization of the primacy of politics.

In the *affluent world* the victory of technology and its subservience to the economic and political powers, with the consequent de-politicizing of large areas of human activity (Marcuse's "one-dimensional man"), resulted in pragmatic man (the producer-consumer) gradually losing control over the "why" of his activity in history. This situation has led to the new primacy of politics in consumer societies: for instance, student protest.

In the *Third World* the struggle for liberation has now gone beyond the ideals of the revolutionary situations of 1789 (France) and 1917 (Russia). In circumstances of a victorious technology in the service of domination on a world scale, the third-world revolution is anti-imperialistic (and, on a national scale, anti-oligarchic) *and* anti-technocratic. It embraces the struggle for a universal share of goods sufficient to ensure basic human dignity, *and* the struggle for free decision-making at all social levels. This gives a new dimension to the primacy of politics; in Latin America this is most evident in resistance to development.

Neo-capitalism's efforts to include its structural contradictions in *models of development* for the Third World are causing a total split in political attitudes to the historical process, and in viewpoints within the Church in Latin America. In comparison with this division, the difference between pre-conciliar traditionalists and post-conciliar reformers (when they concentrate on ecclesial matters and forget politics) is relatively minute. It is almost non-existent compared to that between the latter and those Christians who are really caught up by the urgency of liberation.

Other features of this urgent era of the new primacy of politics stem from circumstances directly affecting Latin America: the vulnerability of its exclusive social systems, with their need for self-preservation; the still relatively primitive organization of society; the chance for dissenting minorities to point out contradictions which the system cannot resolve, and a host of similar factors.

On the foregoing more or less general level, the language used has not yet been markedly political, and therefore lacks the political characteristic of precisely designating power structures and the mechanisms of domination. But there is no point in a political theology that fails to rise to the dialectical challenge of openly naming the components of the infra- and super-structures of power, and the implications of strategic and tactical attacks on them. It is here that European political theology seems to fail: in its language.

5. *The political dimension of faith*

When talking of the political dimension of faith, it is important to remember that it is not something added to the normal content of faith, but the very act of faith in a particular historical context. It is ambiguous simply to speak of the political "consequences" of faith, since this gives a false impression that it is possible to live a life of faith in isolation from daily life, but with the bonus of occasional political "applications".

Faith is no more or less than man's historical activity (which is essentially political). In seeking the basic meaning of his historical existence, man goes so deep into his human "why" that he comes up against the mystery of God working in history, but never outside it. At this point man reaches the mysterious significance of his history at any given time and place, and discovers the relevance of all previous inquiries into the human meaning of history. His capacity to "listen" to the challenges of his history gives him an intuition of what others have previously "listened" to in the same radically historical way. Then he lays himself open to revelation.

Despite the differences from our own world, the most original feature of the socio-cultural world of the Old and New Testaments (in contrast to the Greek world and others) is its setting of the experience of God in the context of man's historical progress. As Metz has pointed out, this means that God in the Bible is the final reference-point for the meaning of human experience on the *socio-political* level, and not on the level of interior personal spirituality.

The transcendence of God consists in the fact that he stands before us on the frontier of the historical future. God is *pro*-vocative — he calls us forwards, and is only to be found as one who goes forward with his people in a constant process of uprooting. Hence the prophets' constant interpretation of God's calls on us in terms of historical and political events.

Jesus and the prophets opposed the cultism and legalism of orthodoxy with the "orthopraxis" of truth made history by means of effective action in the world. Hence the basic characteristic of faith is its historical practice.

In biblical exegesis, political theology lays the stress once again on the meaning of the Exodus as the original principle on which the whole biblical concept of God and faith is based; on the historical and political nature of prophecy; on the prohibition of institutions trying to "capture" God in images; on the shift of the sacred to a point within the humanization of history; and so forth.

In the post-conciliar setting, political theology has insisted on the danger of a new dualism inherent in some reforming tendencies. The more extreme forms of intra-ecclesial reformism, particularly when allied to a-politicism, are victims of a new form of intrinsically anti-biblical dualism. Although the reformers talk much of the world and of service to the world, they are still working within a dualist framework that understands the binomial formula of the Church and world in the sense of "the Church in the world", giving "the world" another reality and seeing its history as "another" history. This is a basic theological issue: the true unitary view of the world cannot see the Church as having a mission to build a separate history, but as the conscious emergence and most explicit living example of the one meaning of the one history.

The Church is wholly "mission": that is, related to the kingdom, which is already foreshadowed in the one history of world salvation. It does not possess in itself (in sociological terms, in its intra-ecclesiastical structures) the point of reference needed to establish the criteria for redirecting its service to the world. Sociologically, this point of reference lies outside its institutional reality. Applied to the notion of the unity of the Church, this means:

> The *locus theologicus* of unity among Christians, lost and sought, is primarily that area "beyond" the world that the Son claims as his domain, and towards the centre of which the Church must constantly strive if it is not to lose its way and betray itself (Metz).

In the light of basic theological principles like this, we now have to examine the implications of the fact that faith must be understood as the historical unfolding of the process of the liberation of man: unfolding in the sense of the truth of faith "becoming true"; liberating efficacy as an integral component of faith; efficacy and gratuitiousness; what can be measured and what cannot in the historical efficacy of love.

6. *From the social to the political in pastoral practice*

There is a "social" Church language, but its vagueness has

now brought it to crisis-point: "the social question", "economic and social justice", "Christian social involvement", and so on.

If its implications were interpreted radically and applied to particular situations, then this social language would lead ineluctably to political awareness and action. But it does not seem to have been strong enough to bring this about.

In the Latin American situation, any pastoral view, as soon as it faces the challenge of the historical process, must have profound political repercussions. This awareness is a distinctive mark of the Christian vanguard in Latin America today.

The old "religious-temporal" dualism still found in many priests and religious, and reinforced by a certain kind of post-conciliar reformism, is at last disappearing.

Pastoral thinking is beginning to take note of the fact that liberating evangelization and the Church's critical and prophetic judgement on social injustice must have political implications; that in the present situation in Latin America pastoral action must have a political bent, or risk leaving the Gospel outside the course of history.

Therefore any elaboration of a political theology to serve such a pastoral practice has to face up to the complexity of the "Church and politics" issue in its implications at *all* levels of Church life. This issue is under discussion throughout Latin America. It cannot be tackled realistically without examining the relationship between the Church and the historical process.

7. Towards a Latin American political theology: the theology of liberation

The historical incidence of the language of "liberation" in the Latin American Church is linked to growing awareness of our situation as oppressed peoples. It began to make its presence strongly felt from 1965 onwards, when theories of development were first disclosed in their true neo-capitalist light. Underlying liberation theology is the historical experience of the actual nature of *under*-development, as a form of dependence. The notion of "liberation" is correlative to that of "development".

A theology of liberation began to take shape only after the Medellín conference, expressed in a series of occasional articles and, more explicitly, in the proceedings of other conferences.4

It took shape as a critical reflection on the historical process of liberation in the sense of faith emerging in action, and appeared as a specifically Latin American form of political theology.

Perhaps the greatest merit of the theology of liberation is its insistence on the starting-point of its reflections: the situation of "dominated (Latin) America". There is a political theology in Latin America today — more spoken than written, it is true — simply because there is a real theology, and because reality is political at its most decisive level. In this theology, to a far greater extent than in the new European political theology, the underlying realities of life in Latin America are becoming intertwined with the basic sources of faith. The Medellín document talks of "liberation" because that is the correct translation of the whole saving message of the gospels. It talks of "a sinful social situation" because that is to date the most complete interpretation of the New Testament (and particularly the Johannine and Pauline) concept of sin. Consequently, terms that relate to the reality of Latin American life — conscientization, imperialism, international markets, monopolies, social classes, development — find their one place in a theology of the highest seriousness.

This insistence on the links between the analysis of underlying realities and the basic sources of faith is one of the main differences between the approach to theology in Latin America and in Europe. And that means a different approach to the nature of political theology.

A political theology cannot become truly aware of critical aspects of faith as a liberating historical process without using analytical language. This brings about a new relationship between theology and the secular sciences. This is one of the basic methodological features of this political theology. There is an enormous difference between a purely descriptive analysis (which predominates in the Medellín documents) and a dialectical-structural analysis, which refers to the causes underlying the mechanics of domination: the choice of analytical instrument itself implies an ethical and political stance.

8. Final note

In my search for an overall view in this brief introductory chapter I have had to stay on a general level. In the following chapters I shall examine the main theological tenets of the "theology of liberation" as expressed in its development to date: the concept of the world as a world in conflict; the relationship between "slavery in Egypt" and the dependent situation of Latin America, between the Exodus and liberation; the history of salvation seen as the salvation of history; a unified vision of creation and redemption; liberating political action and eschatological anticipation; Christ as the mover of history; Christianity and the Church examined in relation to their liberating meaning in history; and the choice for the Church in the 1970s: not development, but liberation.

NOTES

[1] This chapter is based on a lecture given to the Clergy Assembly of Montevideo.

[2] For the various forms taken by "political theology" throughout history, see E. Feil, "Von der 'politischen Theologie' zur 'Theologie der Revolution' ", in E. Feil, R. Weth (eds), *Diskussion zur Theologie der Revolution* (Munich-Mainz, 1969), pp. 82-109.

[3] The term "Third World" is used frequently in this book. But I am aware of its ambiguity. It becomes ideological, in the bad sense of the word, when it is taken as a sociologically valid analytical term. There is no real "Third World", because the countries thought of as making it up are still prevented from forming a cohesive group capable of defending their own interests. They should really be described as *satellites* dominated by one or other of the imperialist blocs; for that is what prevents them from becoming a third world in any true sense. The term also feeds dreams of independence in the absurd sense of cutting off the countries in question from the rest of the world. The best way to understand the expression "Third World" is as a rallying call to the liberation of the dominated and oppressed nations.

4 Multi-national conference in Bogotá, May 1970; ecumenical conference in Buenos Aires, August 1970; international conference in Bogotá, July 1970; and so on.

II Theology of liberation: a prospective evaluation

II Theology of liberation: a prospective evaluation

THIS chapter[1] deals with the impact of an historical experience on Christian awareness. The starting-point is our objective situation as oppressed and dependent peoples, which is forcing itself more and more strongly on the consciousness of broad sections of Christian society in Latin America.

Faced with this situation, all the traditional components of the Christian mentality suddenly seem useless and in need of fundamental re-examination. They belong to an earlier and alien body of experience, and leave the Christians of Latin America with a feeling of abandonment and aloneness, knowing that however benevolently many Christians in the rich countries may look upon this experience, they cannot really share it. Latin American Christians are forced to find their own way. That is our position now. A little lost on our way, some will say — and why not admit it?: "Traveller, there is no path: you make paths by walking". But, lost or not, a creative force is emerging; the people are standing on their own feet, steeling themselves for the historic confrontation that must come.

The aspect of this creative force that concerns us here is its approach to theological reflection. This may not be the most productive aspect at the moment, since the sufferings brought about by the present situation have more dignity, and we can learn more from the human force of actions than from writings that are only relevant when rooted in practice. In Latin America, at least, that is how we usually "do theology", with the result that we have more real than formulated, more spoken than written, theology, which makes it difficult to pick out the main convergent themes with relevance to the actual situation.

Once one accepts the need for study of actual events in all their variety, the limitations of this study become clear: it sets out to be a systematic examination of the constant reference to the theme of "liberation" found in the experience of Latin American Christians today. A fuller study would have to examine all those occasional publications which prompted the appearance of the theme in the communications media. This, in its turn, would lead to a series of secondary studies, because different attitudes have emerged among diverse groups, by virtue of the differing situations in which they find themselves. In addition, despite certain lines of convergence, not all typical Christian attitudes to the subject can be included under common denominators. There are, for example, the "Third-World" group in Argentine, the "Golconda" group in Columbia, the political line of the Montevideo review *Víspera*, and many others. They have all taken a particular stance, and failure to take this into account vitiates most European publications on the subject of the Church in Latin America.[2]

I do not, therefore, propose to analyze the emergence of the theme of "liberation" through particular cases in which it has found special expression, although I shall refer to them occasionally. This involves a certain risk of remaining on a theoretical plane, but does allow a more fundamental investigation of underlying problems common to the various groups, which are otherwise in danger of being passed over; and it is unlikely that outside eyes, however expert — say those of European theologians — will be capable of analyzing these basic problems as they have emerged from our historical experience.

What has been published so far by way of an attempt to explain the "theology of liberation" in fact directly excludes any reference to these basic problems. As Hector Borrat has pertinently remarked: "This reflection takes place in action, in an atmosphere of urgency, and cannot possibly be carried out in academic calm". So it would seem that any attempt to condense the "theology of liberation" into a series of particular themes must mean the elevation to a critical level — whether by theologians or simply Latin American Christians — of much that has previously been latent, half-expressed or just left vague. That elevation is an explicit search for an overall process of reflection, moulded by the originality of our situation as dominated peoples.

I. The historical growth of the "liberation theme"

1. Terminological innovation

Historically, the genesis of the term "liberation" in Latin American Christian writings can be divided into three closely related stages. Before 1965, its appearance was rare, and when it did appear, its meaning was somewhat vague, because the social analysis behind it was vague. It hardly appeared in official church documents: the dominant terminology of the time was generally referred to "development".

In CELAM documents, the language of development enjoyed an almost exclusive hegemony till the eve of the Medellín Conference in 1968. Reference to a "theology of development", expressed as a postulate in the earlier CELAM documents, did give rise to some interesting studies, some trying to take the much-quoted phrase "integral development of man" as their starting-point and put some meat on its bones, and others trying to find a way forward through making the implications of the terminology itself more radical.[3]

From 1965 onwards, the term "liberation" has come into increasing use, particularly in unofficial documents, and the decline of the language of development has been correspondingly hastened. There is an increasing analysis of the phenomenon of under-development, understood ever more clearly as "being kept in a state of under-development", as "a state of dependence", rather than simply the situation of countries "not yet developed" or "in the development phase".

The third phase, marked by the open predominance of the term "liberation" in unofficial documents and its growing use in official ones, came in with the Medellín Conference of 1968, which put the stamp of approval on "liberating" language, using it both in a sociological sense, to describe the situation of "slavery in Egypt" in which our countries find themselves; and, in a theological sense, relating it closely to salvation and its correlatives. In the document on education, the term acquired a certain methodology and a programme as "liberating education", linked to Paulo Freire's theme of "conscientization".

After Medellín, the word "liberation" occurs with impressive frequency in episcopal documents, particularly those of the hierarchies that made a real effort to apply the conclusions of the conference to the situation in their own countries. It appears in titles of documents — "The Gospel and the Liberation of Man", by the Chilean bishops, for example, — in thematic contexts — "salvation-liberation", "grace-liberation", and as an adjective: "liberating pastoral practice". Along with the other key word "conscientization", it dominates the ecclesiastical language of the time.

This summing-up of linguistic innovation prompts the question whether this is just a process of open verbal catharsis amidst the general desuetude of traditional ecclesiastical language, or whether even its more indiscriminate use shows a positive break — a shift of the semantic axis of this language.[4]

2. Sociological and semantic content

The susceptibility of Christian media to verbal magic, to the verbosity of proclamation, is an established fact: we are easily tempted to a "presence through the word", devoid of follow-up action. The roots of this inclination to a mere verbal debauch are probably to be found in the material base (infrastructure) which, historically, conditioned the ideological superstructure of the Church — the understanding of power that conditioned the notion of the efficacy of the word, seen at its height in the *ex opere operato* of sacramentalism removed from its real historical preconditions, for example.

Of course there is a lot of this proclamatory verbosity, without any real foundation on the practical level, in the growth of the liberation theme, but I do not think that is sufficient to explain its sudden appearance and dynamic growth, particularly when one takes account of the sociological content it presupposes.

"Liberation", taken as much in the sense of "acquiring" as of "recovering" liberty, is always a notion referring to a present lack of liberty, thereby involving a clear judgment on, and condemnation of, the present state of affairs.

Through its refusal to accept what exists, the very notion implies a judgment: it is a word of *confrontation* and *conflict*. Of course this must not be exaggerated: one cannot presuppose the existence of a detailed analytical judgment on, say, the phenomenon of under-development, behind every use of the word, which simply implies a general condemnation of the existing state of affairs and the need for change. On its own, it can be either reforming or revolutionary, depending on the analytical content underlying its use. Content is the area to concentrate on.

In common Christian usage, the introduction of the term "liberation" implies a *dislocation of the semantic axis of the word "liberty"*. This is of paramount importance, because it is a concrete example of the ideological and semantic domination and imprisonment of our language. Even progressive European theology is still sull of talk about "liberty", but totally neglects the term "liberation"; this is probably the fault of our translations of the Bible. The historic mentality of Judaeo-Christianity, in contrast to the cosmic fixity of Greek thought, was one of process, practice and change; but how does one insist on that if the terms used in biblical translations are abstract, a-historical, postulatory terms, and not situational or process words — words that explicate practice? That is the significance of the Latin-American theological attempt to regain the historical and dynamic force of the biblical vocabulary by using the word "liberation".

In essence, the precise term "liberation" subverts the magical and proclamatory structure of "action through the word" (Ger.: *Worttat*) and replaces it by "the word of action" (Ger.: *Tatwort*). It aims at the historical growth of liberty as a political reality, and it contradicts the semantic bases of the vague liberal idea of "rights to freedom".

To appreciate the importance of this semantic upheaval, one has only to reflect that official church language is still struggling to assimilate the vaguely provocative content of the liberal revolution (the "rights of man", and so on).

These, of course, are only general considerations, and may be of some importance in relation to the ideological domination of the conventional language of theology and pastoral care. They indicate that the terminological innovation in Latin-America must be something more than a mere tactical recourse to seductive terminology, and more than just a slogan for a theology threatened with extinction. But what is its root content?

3. Liberation and dependence

The mere extension of the use of "liberating" terms in Christian media, and particularly the attempt to establish immediate connexions of a theological nature — "liberation-salvation", and so on — can easily give the impression that this language is a spontaneous product of the climate of reform after the second Vatican council.

That this is not the case is indicated first by the fact that the European post-conciliar vanguard has not adopted it; and, second, by the general criticism levelled by users of the language of liberation at the "reformists" for their ecclesial introversion. This, of course, is not to deny that that language has found a precise correlation with some basic elements in Christianity, but it is not sufficient to examine the niceties of theological and pastoral language to find the greatest influence on the use of the term "liberation".

The various movements of national liberation, for example, have exercised a far more direct influence. The language of the revolutionary movements of the Left, the Marxist vocabulary of Latin American "new Marxism" (which is different from the reformist approach of the Communist parties that follow the Moscow line), the terms used by student movements: all these had a more or less direct influence. So, to a certain extent, did the writings of Herbert Marcuse (though somewhat less in Latin America than elsewhere) and documents from international congresses on "the dialectics of liberation".

These, however, are no more than formal elements expressing a state of consciousness which originates in a harsh discovery: the revelation of the workings of domination that keep us in an underdeveloped state. Underlying them is the major event of an *historical experience raised to a conscious level*. We are beginning to realize what we are in history: not merely underdeveloped peoples in the sense of "not yet sufficiently developed", but peoples "kept in a state of underdevelopment": dominated and oppressed peoples — which is a very different thing.

The 1960s were a decade of successive frustrations for Latin America: the failure of the Alliance for Progress; the engineered undermining of ALALC; the growing imperialist control of organizations supposed to be helping development (OEA, CEPAL, CIES, CIAP, BID, AID, and so on); the impossibility of making even our most modest demands heard on the international scene (meetings of GATT, UNCTAD, CECLA, in 1969, and so forth); the militarization of the Continent, the setting-up of powerful structures of repression with the open and direct support of the CIA; and the massive influx of foreign capital with its consequent removal of industrial development from national control and misdirection of industrialization.

It is this situation of cumulative frustration that has given rise to *critical opposition to development models* which are generally *cul-de-sacs*, although in some cases they could mitigate the structural contradictions of capitalism, but even then could not carry the bulk of the population with them, as in the case of Brazil and Argentine. The excessive price paid for "development" is the growing alienation of large sectors of the community and the repression of all forms of protest.

Now that the concept of "development" has been shown up for the lie that is is, "losing its technical meaning to acquire a connotation of political ideology",[5] the acceptance or rejection of the theories behind it has become a *criterion for differentiation* between political attitudes. This applies to Christian as well as secular thought, and is the cause of the tremendous complexity and radicality of the current internal divisions in the Church in Latin America, which it would be ingenuous to try to minimize.

Rooted as it is in the present historical context of Latin America, the theological and political theme of liberation is the obvious correlative of the sociological theme of "dependence". Just as the latter marks the beginning of a new line in social science in Latin America, breaking away from the scientific methodology and "theoretical models" imported from North American and European schools,[6] which were incapable of facing up to the complexity and political connotation of the problem in this form, so the theological and political theme of liberation ushers in a *new context* and a *new methodology* of Christian reflection on faith as a definite historical event.

4. Criteria for differentiation in the use of the language of liberation

The term "liberation" is now in wide use in the Christian media of the Continent. Although its origins lie in the realization of our situation as dominated peoples, its increasingly indiscriminate use requires that certain criteria of differentiation be established. In other words, this is a complete phenomenon, containing in itself the dialectic of different levels of the one basic empirical fact: our situation as dominated peoples.

Use of the same language obviously does not always imply the presence of the same level of appreciation of the historical reality underlying it. The Medellín documents, for example, contain many elements of criticism of "developmentism", and even reveal a basically "anti-development" stance — particularly in the document on élites — but their overall tone is vague, not only because of lack of definition in the objectives of the hierarchical representatives whose voice they are, but also above all because of the type of analysis (more descriptive than dialectical and structural) that they use. Furthermore, the documents go beyond the normal pastoral practice of their authors in their dioceses.

Taken as a whole, the language of liberation implies a need to *go beyond the language of development*, introduces a *new polarization of thought and action*, and contains at least the germ of a *new judgment* on reality and a *new experience* of conflictive confrontation. Consequently, even when it remains vague and fails to express attitudes that should follow from its new analytical content, it retains a tremendous overall function of increasing self-awareness, because it serves as a buttress to particular positions. Furthermore, it would be unrealistic and even disrespectful to expect terminological innovations to take on an immediately unanimous meaning.

The criteria for establishing the levels on which this language is assimilated have a common point of reference in the degree of perception of the non-viability of the "development" option, whose "crisis" (judgment) gave rise to the terminology. In other words, the way in which the mechanics of "dependence" was interpreted, the depth of the analysis of the phenomenon of underdevelopment and the stances adopted in regard to it, determine the degree of precision with which the language of liberation is used. Whether or not these are theological or non-theological criteria for determining the validity of the historic language of faith depends on what one understands by theology, and how the theology of liberation measures up to that understanding.

II. First steps in the theology of liberation

1. Sources of information

Historically speaking, the explicit formulation of a "theology of liberation" is of recent date; it was part of the emergence of the "liberating" language we have just been discussing, and an attempt to reflect critically on the Christian implications of this new language. The term "theology of liberation" is now widely used to indicate theological aspects of the "dependence-liberation" formula.

The Medellín Conference gave rise to a large and increasing number of documents on the "theology of liberation", many of them journalistic and without pretension to theological depth, which meant that many of them dated rapidly. Many other, more basic, articles expressed the urgent need for a theology of liberation.

For those who require a theology which answers to rigid scientific criteria, these occasional pieces are of little moment. But, if applied to Latin America, such rigid criteria would ignore significant aspects of a fundamental change of heart among Christians. In fact the very number and diversity of these manifestos, articles, essays based on experience, and similar documents make them one of the most effective demonstrations of the vitality of the vanguard of the Latin-American Church.

With their growing realization of the *originality of their historical experience as dominated peoples*, the Christians of Latin America are increasingly sure that the priorities of the "progressive" theology of the developed world are irrelevant to their needs.

The influence of Teilhard de Chardin, valuable for its emphasis on historical reality, soon exhausted its potential. The initial Christian-Marxist dialogue, as practised in the developed countries, seemed to avoid any direct confrontation with the real needs of the historical moment. The reforms initiated by Vatican II took an almost exclusively intra-ecclesial turn. "Secularization theology" became a cult, but remained basically ambiguous and for the most part politically naive; it never had any real relevance to the Latin American situation. Still less did the "death of God" theology, which often showed an uncritical acceptance of the "one-dimensional" and de-politicized man of the affluent society. Even the more specialized approach of the "theology of revolution" or "theology of violence" failed to be wide enough and at the same time specific enough to take account of the urgency of the situation in Latin America.

All these different schools may have provided insights that helped to build up a new state of self-awareness, but historical experience of the unrelenting forces of domination was a much stronger influence. More than anything else, the personal experience of belonging to dominated nations has produced the theology of liberation.

After the accumulated frustrations of the "first decade of development", 1970 was the first year in which conferences and symposia on the theme of "theology of liberation" became commonplace throughout Latin America. Some of the major ones were:

An international symposium on the theology of liberation held in Bogotá from 2-7 March 1970. Two publications resulted, one preparatory, the other publishing the papers read.[7] A co-ordinating centre was established and a duplicated bulletin entitled *Theology of Liberation* containing documentation and reflective essays was started.

An ecumenical seminar on the theme of theology of liberation held in Buenos Aires from 3-6 August 1970, with twenty theologians attending, and repeated the following year.

After a series of regional meetings, the Bogotá Symposium was repeated from 24-26 July 1970, this time concentrating on under-development as a form of dependence.

Another seminar was held in Ciudad Juárez, Mexico, from 16-18 October 1970, with Harvey Cox and other internationally-known theologians taking part. Some of the talks given at this were immediately distributed throughout Latin America.

A group of biblical scholars met in Buenos Aires in July 1970 to discuss the subject "Exodus and Liberation", and many of the papers were published in *Revista Biblíca*.

A theological and pastoral symposium held at Oruro in Bolivia in December 1970 concentrated on the theology of liberation, with nine papers on the subject.

At CELAM level, the meeting of Presidents and Secretaries of the Episcopal Education Commission, held at Medellín from 27 August to 2 November, included a long paper on the subject, given by the General Secretary of CELAM.[8]

These examples, which deliberately omit all purely national and regional meetings, will give some idea of the way the subject rapidly acquired widespread importance in Latin America. At the same time, popular articles and essays multiplied rapidly, extending even to the daily and weekly Press. Obviously, there was much repetition, and it is more important to pick out salient themes than to try to produce an exhaustive list.

2. *The basic concept: the dependence-liberation formula*

One thing virtually all the documents so far published agree on is that the starting-point of the theology of liberation is the present historical situation of domination and dependence in which the countries of the Third World find themselves. Criticism of the "development" option through an analysis of its failures has been the typical approach to reflection on its implications for Christians.

The idea of "liberation" cannot, of course, be tied to this particular context, but it does serve as a starting-point, not only because we are looking for a "Latin American theology" (which is one of the reasons), but because this is the situation of two-thirds of humanity and as such must impinge on the historical consciousness of Christianity and pose radical questions about the nature of the Church's mission.

The starting-point is by no means a local Latin American phenomenon, and the task for theology is not one of local importance only. Of course it has to look at this particular situation, but it must do more than that: if the state of domination and dependence in which two-thirds of humanity live, with an annual toll of thirty million dead from starvation and malnutrition, does not become the starting-point for *any* Christian theology today, even in the affluent and powerful countries, then theology cannot begin to relate meaningfully to the real situation. Its questions will lack reality and not relate to real men and women. As one speaker at the Buenos Aires Seminar observed, "we have to save theology from its cynicism". When one looks at the real problems of the world today, much theological writing can only be called cynical.

> There was a time when the Church responded to the questions asked of it with an imperturbable appeal to its doctrinal and institutional traditions. Today, the problem we call liberation is so serious and so widespread that it calls both Christianity and the Church in question. They are being asked to demonstrate their significance when faced with a human problem of such magnitude.[9]

If under-development has to be described as not mere backwardness but a form of dependence, then *all Christians have to find a new approach*: "Because the decade of the development option is over and we have entered the decade of liberation. Because liberation is the new name of development".[10]

Taking this historical situation as the starting-point for reflection on the Christian faith does not mean that the concept of liberation has to be restricted to the economic plane, but it is on this plane that the priorities become dramatically obvious:

> The liberation of man throughout history implies not only better living conditions, radical structural change, social revolution, but much more: the continuous creation of a new way of being human, a permanent cultural revolution.[11]

The starting-point we are taking is definite in its relevance to a situation and open-ended in its structural implications. Definite, because it starts from the Latin American situation: "My starting-point is this: dominated (Latin) America".[12] Open-ended, because once it criticizes the concept of "development" for being too narrow in human terms, it replaces it by the concept of "liberation" as more expressive both of the aspirations of the oppressed and the fulness of a liberating perspective: "Conceiving history as a process of man's liberation situates the social changes we want to bring about in a dynamic context and broadens their horizon. At the same time, it enables us better to understand the times we are living in".[13]

The term "liberation" can be applied on three levels: the political liberation of oppressed nations and social classes; the liberation of mankind throughout the course of history; and liberation from sin, the cause of all evil, preparing the way for a life of all mankind in communion with the Lord. This last aspect indicates why theology finds more meaning in this term than in "development":

> The term "development" somewhat clouds the theological questions implicit in the process, while talking of "liberation" leads more directly to the biblical sources that inspire man's presence and action in history: liberation from sin and the bringing of a new life by Christ the Saviour.[14]

Politically and theologically, "liberation" is more exact, gives better expression to the conflictive nature of the process and is richer in its implications, besides offering a richer field for theological reflection.

There is of course a danger in opening its meaning out to this extent, of depriving it of its strength at the level of practical tactics and strategy. At the Bogotá Symposium, there were those who claimed that talking of liberation was evasion. Then why the pretension of "taking this subject out of the realm of the taboo"?[15] I think there is a valid warning here: not for a moment should its analytical content or central semantic axis be forgotten; any discussion of liberation must always go back to its essence: denouncing domination; perception of the mechanics of dependence; opposition to "development" and the capitalist economic system; and a break with the "unjust established order".

III. Methodological aspects

1. In what sense is this "theology"?

One of the basic aspects of the new Latin American theological attitude is its criticism of theology itself — even of the "progressive" theology of the affluent nations. Yet those who look for systematic, analytically-formulated criticism will be disappointed. They are justified in claiming that such diffuse and only partially expressed criticism is still unsure of itself and has not yet really fully worked out its own position. We Latin Americans must accept the strength of this objection, but at the same time we have a right to reply that this does not alter the fact of the existence of this criticism, or invalidate its insights.

This criticism has now become a state of mind. Inevitably, however negative such an approach may be, it is sometimes aggressive and sometimes presumptuous. The psychological effort involved in eradicating the "parasite me" from "the mind of the oppressor injected into the mind of the oppressed" (Paulo Freire) is not a smooth process. This is not the place to examine the "pedagogy of the oppressed" (Freire) which is something that Latin American theologians experience as a personal process. As Joseph Comblin has said: "Any Latin American who has studied in Europe has to undergo detoxification before he can begin to act".

The form this criticism takes can best be described by describing some typical cases. At the Buenos Aires meeting, J. L. Segundo analyzed various aspects of the difference in theological approach between the affluent world and the Third World. One of the defects of the former is its basic leaning to idealism and consequent inability to be historically realistic. Its questions do not spring from the basic conflict inherent in the real situation; they idealize reality. Schools like the "death of God" theology are a non-political accommodation to the pragmatism of the consumer society. The "secularization" theme, as expressed in Europe and the United States, concentrates almost exclusively on the desacralization brought into the man-nature relationship by technology, and ignores the primordial (political) aspects of the man-nature-man relationship, the man-mechanics of the domination relationship, and the whole question of "principalities and powers". The contribution made by a "theology of liberation" springing from the reality of dominated nations could be a radical approach to the political aspects of the "secularization" theme: an all-out attack on "order" and the "powers" that hold man in subjugation.

Other aspects generally criticized in Latin America are: the horrifying political reaction latent in insensibility to the political dimension of the problems — as in the case of Hans Küng; the inability of many "progressive" exegetes to play with "suspicions" — Marx was called "a master of suspicions" — related to the real priorities, or to generate hypotheses which might transform the *status quo*; the abstract "historicity" of the vast bulk of post-conciliar theology supposedly based on the history of salvation — as evidenced in *Mysterium Salutis*, for example; and an excessively vague sociological content, linked to an inability to use real examples, as in Moltmann's *Theology of Hope* or Metz's *Political Theology*. Some journals, such as the review *Víspera*, have gone so far as to make criticism of "nordic" or "North Atlantic" theology a constant ingredient of their subject matter.

The basic point at issue here is how to redefine the meaning of theology in the context of liberation. The first attempt was made by Gustavo Gutiérrez, who has outlined an interpretation of the different sociological and ideological functions exercised by theology throughout its history.[16] When we talk of theology today, we cannot suppose a neutral bond between theology and faith in each period of history: there is always a political aspect to the way in which theology is made. This point needs emphasizing, because the political dimension has never been absent — least of all at times when theology seemed to concentrate solely on reaching the limits of personal spirituality — because this very lack of political content reflects the influence of a reactionary and alienating political ideology.[17] So the notions of a "spiritual" or "scientific" theology are ambiguous in themselves, though to stress this does not imply any antipathy toward spirituality or science, but merely the need to point out that they obscure the ideological or political role that such theologies have played in the past and play today.

There is something particularly original about this criticism, which is heard in Europe too, although there the problem it implies and the denunciation it contains are still far from the consciousness of the still dominant sectors of Christian theology. The real step forward only comes with a demand for all theology to concentrate on the historical reality of men's actions (particularly those of Christians) in transforming the world, to such an extent that this becomes a constant point of reference. To do this, theology must abandon the residual ingenuousness with which it approaches its real function, which always has a political content. It has to realize, consciously, the impossibility of avoiding its relation to practice, because when it tries to avoid this, perhaps in the name of a scientific objectivity devoid of ideological content, it fails, since the very process of avoidance takes on a depoliticizing ideological function. This in itself is an eminently political function, definitely connected with practice, but in this case in defence of the *status quo*.

The choice of titles is indicative of differences in this context: in Europe one can publish articles on "The Place of Theology in Society"; in Latin America the approach is more direct: "From Society to Theology".[18] The subject matter is much the same; the starting-point and approach are quite different. The phrases typical of the Latin American approach may not satisfy the requirements of absolute precision, but they are indicative of a particular way of approaching theology: "Theology deals with particular events", "springs from reality", "is not a pure, intellectual exercise, but an act of commitment"; it has to be "basically critical and basically prophetic" — to "let itself be questioned by reality"; no one can be a theologian without "being in touch with reality, without suffering in a certain way", and so on.

Gutiérrez insists on the "primacy of action", on liberating action as a "*locus theologicus*". Theology follows practice and forms part of it as a "critical reflection on action". It is the second act, action being the first, even for the theologian. When this leads to a definition of theology as "critical reflection on the pastoral action of the Church", it is vital to avoid seeing in this a simple repetition of the more general recent conception of pastoral theology found in the works of Schuster, Rahner, and others. They concentrate almost exclusively on action inside the Church, the general concern of post-conciliar reformism, while the theology of liberation shifts the emphasis toward liberating action, in a strongly political sense, in the context of the conflict situation of the world today. This is clear in the affirmation that pastoral action, which is really considered relevant and therefore as the proper object of critical reflection, is not any sort of "presence in the world", but "the major fact of this presence in our time, above all in the under-developed countries, the participation of Christians in the struggle to build a just, fraternal society, in which men can live with dignity and be agents of their own destiny".[19] Hence there is a central point of reference.

2. *Theology and secular sciences*

We come back to the previous question: Are we not establishing non-theological criteria for deciding the degree of validity of the historical language of faith? Why call critical reflection on historical experience "theology" when it is already being done, perhaps more competently, by sociologists, historians, political scientists, social philosophers, and others? What makes this sort of inquiry theological?

Latin American writings contain only a vague answer to these questions. The actual debate, until now about different ways of looking at reality, is not usually so direct, which makes sense in that it shows that theology is intended as an expression of the hope of liberation, not as a theoretical debate to define hope. European readers will have to find their own way through the maze, to pick out the methodological clarifications to be found here and there. And no one will deny that there are still many things that need to be made clearer.

But there are answers too: first, the centrality of reference to the liberating experience of Christians. This may not be sufficient to raise critical reflection to the level of theology, as religious sociology uses the same reference point. But there is a difference, found in the use of such phrases as: "the historical embodiment of faith", "in the light of the gospel", "in the light of revelation", by "liberation" theologians describing this experience.

Yet, could this difference be merely a sort of short-circuit, juxtaposing criteria of faith on one hand — criteria already established and ready to be plucked out at the opportune moment —, with, on the other, the demand that such criteria respond to the situational context of experience, that they spring from reality? In other words, isn't theology trying to speak from the basis of the gospels, of revelation, of the essence of Christianity, and at the same time from the secular sciences, elevating their data as prime facts and indispensable sources of reference?

The question becomes even more complicated when one takes a hard look at the fact that "Christian faith", "the gospels" and "revelation" do not exist as realities (or criteria) that can be clearly adduced in themselves; they exist only in the form that history has handed down to us.

Constant allusions to the primacy of the event, to facts, to the historical forms of Christianity, and the deformations they involve, are an exact indication of this acute consciousness that we do not possess Christianity "as such" in a way that enables us to introduce it into discussion as an *a priori* critical criterion. This is particularly true in Latin America, where criticism of the supportive role of the Church in relation to the *status quo* is constant among committed Christians.

It is impossible to go straight to the "heart of Christianity" because Christianity exists only in a series of historical embodiments; if the Bible itself is not a direct source of criteria, but the history of successive interpretations, always partial and sometimes directly contradictory, of these criteria; if the conjuncture of word and deed is essential to the concept of revelation; and if, furthermore, all this has come down to us formed, deformed, reformed and deformed yet again by the actual history of Christianity; and if the differing historical circumstances in which Christianity has found itself have produced their own formulations of dogma, canon law and pastoral practice; then how can we talk simply of criteria perceived "in the light of faith"? How can we talk candidly of the "gospel" when there is so much truth in what one committed Christian once said to me: "The Bible? It doesn't exist. The only Bible is the sociological bible of what I see happening here and now as a Christian"?

There is a hermeneutical problem that can be left for later discussion, but it does call for some immediate observations. First: When Latin Americans make apparently simplistic connexions with the contents or criteria of the gospels or Christian faith, that is not because they are ignoring, or ignorant of, the complexity of the question of what can be considered Christian or not. Their realization of this complexity is evident from their basic questioning of the historical embodiment of Christianity in their midst. It would be unfair to discuss the force of this critique and confrontation, and its significance in terms of a critical understanding of the whole historical existence of Christianity, including early Christianity. De-toxification is a necessary process.

The appeal to faith and the gospel cannot be interpreted simply as naive fundamentalism, although that is a danger imposed by the so-called "Christian" socio-cultural climate of the Continent (with the possible exception of Uruguay) — a fact that sets it apart from the rest of the Third World.

This brings us to the complex problem of the relationship between the vanguard of committed Christians and "popular religiosity". The way — or rather "ways", since they are obviously not all of the same mind — in which they tackle this problem is one of the most significant aspects of their refusal to be bound by European clichés. On the one hand, because popular religion exists, it cannot be dismissed by despising it or criticizing it *in toto*. On the other, it is a deeply ambiguous phenomenon and cannot be approached uncritically or simply used as a tactical weapon.

The theological expressions have to be seen in the context of this very real and particular dialectics. One must frankly admit the danger of making direct connexions between theological data and the sociological data of an ambiguously "Christian" socio-cultural climate. But as long as this "theological immediacy" serves the critical consciousness of the people, it cannot be dismissed as uncritical.

It is neither possible, not historically opportune, to try to take all the steps in one bound. If we were now to concentrate on showing our awareness of all the critical considerations, all the "ifs" and "buts", we could be escaping from the priorities of the situation. These must be critically analyzed as a whole, and in this context a simple Yes in relation to the connexion with this or that criterion of faith is not just a seductive use of language or theological adornment, but a critical approach turned into the language of experience. The great danger here is exercising the mind of the most thoughtful Christians of the Continent very strongly at the present time, because they see that historical realism can easily be reduced to superficial criticism.

The succinct "in the light of faith" and similar phrases have, in fact, a much deeper meaning than that of simple viability: in the Latin American context, they serve to guide a critical consciousness. They become the distinctive characteristic of theology.

Critical reflection on human history becomes theological to the degree that it looks for the presence of the Christian faith in historical experience; it is this that distinguishes theology from other ways of reflecting critically on this experience. If reference to faith in history is laid aside, then there is no theology. In this sense, "in the light of faith", "in the light of revelation", and so on – for all the questions they leave unanswered – denote the essence of theological reflection.

Note that this is the typical characteristic of theology, not its sole preoccupation. The theology of liberation takes a decisive step in the direction of the secular sciences by admitting that the fact of human experience, on which the secular sciences have the first word to say, is its basic point of reference, its contextual starting-point. One might say that, by defining itself as critical reflection based on the inner meaning of the process of liberation, the theology of liberation can be seen not only as the "second act" after the "first act" of action, but as the "second word" after the "first word" of the secular sciences — which is not to be understood as presuming to be the "last word". In a way it is, for those who believe in Christ, but in view of theology's habitual disregard for the secular sciences, that would be a dangerous general claim to make.

In this context, the methodology of *Gaudium et Spes*, so different from that of the other conciliar documents, became paradigmatic for Latin American theology. It was a first sign that the secular sciences were being taken seriously as providing data for theological reflection.[20] This had still not become widespread in Europe, but it is standard practice in Latin America, where theology starts *only* from an analysis of reality and usually takes a tripartite form: analysis of reality, theological reflection, and pastoral considerations. This is a conscious methodological innovation often noted in articles on the theology of liberation.

The objection made to the "sociologization of theology" does not really affect us, because it would seem to assume the impossible postulate of a theology that did *not* take analysis of reality as made by the secular sciences as its starting-point. Impossible, not merely because we say so, but because their "theological purism" cannot stand up to contact with the Bible; exegesis cannot dispense with the secular sciences in its attempt to reach the true meaning of the biblical texts. When it tries to do so, it not only fails to get to grips with the real challenge of the Bible, but — much worse — fails to make the biblical text speak in a meaningful way to the problem-laden men of today.

If it is to benefit from the serious methodological procedures that prompt the most acute questions, it should perhaps be less jealous of its special nature. Such questions are: what is the most appropriate scientific instrument the secular sciences can provide for investigating the human and political aspects of problems? What sort of ethical and political choice should appear in the selection of the appropriate methodology for investigating the human elements in historical experience? Here again, the intrinsic value of experience has to be taken into account as an essential ingredient of scientific investigation, and science has to be aware of the ideological implications hiding under the name of "scientific neutrality". In view of the appalling political naiveté of much theology, it can at least be suggested that using secular science as a basis for theological reflection may be the only realistic way of dragging theology out of its ghetto.

To sum up: for critical reflection on human history to become theology, it must have the distinctive characteristic of reference to faith and the historical embodiments of this faith — the Bible and the history of Christianity. But "purely theological" criteria are not sufficient if they are criteria drawn from the supposedly exclusive resources of theology. Firstly: because they are not clear in themselves — they have to be "made to speak", even as texts, through the secular sciences; secondly: because they are even less adequate if used to relate the "word" to the facts of present-day human experience.

This means, paradoxically, that the distinctive characteristic of theology — its reference to faith and its historical witness — is not enough to distinguish good theology from bad. To make this distinction requires added criteria of reference to the historical value of experience, such as the process of liberation in history, and these can only be formed through the secular sciences. Evangelization, whose handmaid theology is, should be the historical articulation of love-in-practice, not the mere enunciation of a message. In the Bible, no message is valid unless it "is made true" in practice. So theology must necessarily look to the secular sciences, even to find out what distinguishes it from them.

IV. Common lines of theological exposition

This section sets out the themes that at present appear most frequently in writings on the theology of liberation, though perhaps "indications" might be a better description than "themes", as they are generally indications of a way to begin rather than fully-developed expositions. In originality and depth they are very modest as yet, but they have the originality of never losing sight of the situation of oppression from which they spring, and of always being practical.

1. The world as conflict

This is a constant rather than an occasional theme. The lack of reference to the real situation of conflict, with its strong political connotations, in most post-conciliar writing is often fiercely criticized. A realistic vision of the world today would leave no room for optimism, while the ghetto-like withdrawal of many sectors of the Church has conditioned people to take an ingenuous view, proposing facile forms of conciliation between the "Church and the world" — an outworn phrase that should be replaced by "Church in the world" or "Church of the world". They think nothing of falling back on the old "flight within", but that is only possible through a resolution of the struggle with the world as it exists.[21]

The recent history of Latin America demonstrates that the world is not naturally open to change. On the contrary, we are witnessing a closing of ranks against change, and a climate of mounting repression. The notions of organic change coming about through a "naturally open society", as found in T. Parsons, W. Buckley, *et al*, need to be opposed.

But the conflict in the world cannot be considered in the abstract. Its mechanics have to be named: repression, false harmonization, and so on. Such analytical terms, which can always be improved on, are needed to express the basic biblical themes of conflict, judgment, sin, and so forth.

> Terms that describe the infrastructure (of Latin American society) become, in their own right, part of the terminology of the most serious theology: conscientization, imperialism, international market, social classes, development . . .[22]

Certainly the Council Fathers could not foresee the complexity and ambiguities to which this confrontation between the Church and the world was to give rise in Latin America. There the word "world" does not mean — as it might in Europe — a place in which the history of man unfolds peacefully . . . There, the "world" is increasingly a battlefield on which the conflict is becoming more and more general . . .[23]

2. Slavery in Egypt and Exodus

The biblical motif of the Exodus is mentioned with impressive frequency, with a correlation between "the freeing of Israel and the hour of Latin America" being made in reference to the actual process of liberation, as in the introduction to the Medellín documents. The symbolism of the "plagues of Egypt" is linked to the process of conscientization. The promises are found in the struggle.

> The Exodus was the experience that moulded the consciousness of the people of Israel. It became the structuring principle that determined its way of organizing its time and space. It is not just something in the consciousness of Israel: if it were, it would be just another piece of information. It is more than that; it is the structuring principle because it determined the logic with which Israel assimilated the facts of its historical experience, and the principle by which it organized them and interpreted them. The Exodus did not remain as a past experience, something that happened at a particular time in a particular place. It became the paradigm for the interpretation of all space and all time.[24]

Institutions do not usually model themselves on this structuring principle of the Exodus: they more normally regard themselves as "epiphanic", as upholders of fulfilled promises. It is difficult to see how institutions can come to embody the critical consciousness, the permanent cultural revolution structured on the axis of the continual struggle for liberation, that is the mark of exodus as a permanent motif.

We have to beware of a sort of "exodus triumphalism" in references to a "liberating exodus" when there is no experience of any such thing in a country's history. It is doubtful if we do have any real examples of attempted exodus as a means to freedom; if Metz's "subversive memory" really forms a part of our collective subconscious; if the "freedom fighters" of the past, often now peacefully enshrined in the parthenons of national memory, have any real relevance to the present situation.

3. A world in conflict: institutionalized violence; sin

The Medellín document speaks of the "social situation" of sin, because this is at present the most apt interpretation of the New Testament (particularly the Pauline and Johannine) concept of sin.

Although the personal dimension of responsibility has to be emphasized, the situation in Latin America is a clear example of the social dimension of sin enshrined in particular events.

4. Liberation-salvation

This is the most common theological theme. Now that the purely "salvationist" understanding of the Church's mission in the world has been superseded, "the unvarnished affirmation of the possibility of universal salvation has radically changed the way we look at the Church's mission in the world . . . the Church now seeks a new and radical service of mankind".[25]

The concept of salvation has been historicized to the point where one has to ask the question: "Saved in this world or the next?". That is, horizontalism versus verticalism — and all the variations on this opposition are equally expressive in the context of the new emphasis. The old dualisms of natural-supernatural, nature-grace, and so on, no longer express opposites, and the same is true of the old Protestant doctrine of the "two kingdoms" and "two orders", whose roots go so deep.

5. History of salvation or salvation of history?

Segundo formulated the question in this provocative way, designed to show up the actual a-historicity of much current theology. Obviously the two should not be seen as opposites, and Gutiérrez insists that "the struggle for a just society is fully and rightfully part of saving history".[26]

6. Creation and the salvation process of liberation

The only Christological meaning of creation and salvation

(Col 1: 15-20) is summed up in the phrase "creation of a new man", which is so close to the spirit of many revolutionary writings today: "When we state that man realizes his potential in prolonging the work of creation through his labour, we mean that by virtue of this fact he places himself inside the process of saving history. Building the earthly city is not a simple stage of 'humanization', or 'pre-evangelization', as the theology of a few years ago used to have it; it is integrating oneself fully in a saving process that embraces all mankind".[27]

Such statements should be understood not only in the sense of referring to labour in the technical sense, but in a context of political struggle; that is why the "theologies of work", "theologies of earthly realities" and others typical of the technical world — which have been called "appendix theologies" — are so ingenuous and inadequate.

7. Liberating political presence and eschatological hope

In the context of a Christianity still very polarized by the "further dimension of history", the critical element in the eschatological dimension of Christianity needs to be stressed. The challenges of the present have made the old formulations ("applied eschatology", "present eschatology", and so on) lose their capacity for defining and expressing the dialectic between the "kingdom" that has already arrived and that which is to come. They have therefore lost their usefulness to the Christian today, whose hallmark is above all to embody the hope that is in him in experience and witness in particular historical situations (1 Pet 3:15).

The dialectical polarity set up by eschatological "dissatisfaction" on account of what is not yet an effective anticipation of what can and should be, disqualifies the Christian from any form of accommodation to the *status quo*.

If the final eschatological vision isn't made operative, and doesn't become a practical articulation of hope, it is a pretext for evading the facts of history. The political aspect of eschatology is therefore an important recurring theme in the theology of liberation.

8. Christ the animator of history

Christology, it is generally agreed, is one of the most urgent tasks facing theology today, and also one of its worst gaps. For the moment, not surprisingly, the theology of liberation has not offered any improvement on the current slogans: Christ present in history, the resurrected Lord animating history, Christ identified with the outsider and the poor, and so forth.

If this affirmation of the presence of Christ in the historical process is to be more than an ideological substitute for the irreplaceable commitment of every individual to the struggle for liberation; if it is to be more than a "pure fable", a conciliatory proclamation evading the real contradictions of the world, it must not be presented as something completely ethereal, or as a mere identification with specific movements or persons involved in the process of liberation.

On the one hand, there has to be a possibility of a real connexion between this Christ, working through us, and the process of liberation; on the other, this Christ has to be always challenging, a prophet and a liberator, one who judges, condemns, and provokes, calls us forward, introducing a dialectic into the process.

9. The significance of Christianity

One of the important contributions made by the theology of liberation is its insistence on the new challenge facing Christians as a result of the situation of oppression in which two-thirds of humanity exist. That means that Christians have to re-think their mission in the world. This can no longer be seen as belonging to the personal sphere, as the various derivations of existentialism current in theology would have us believe, nor can it be simply an ecclesiastical affair of looking out from the Church on to the world, as has been the dominant tendency in some areas of post-conciliar reform (which have spent their energies on such unproductive preoccupations as internal reforms in the Church).

Once it sets itself fully in the broad context of the world and allows itself to be challenged by the needs of human history, Christianity will find its special significance in the rediscovery of the implications of the historical dialectic contained in its eschatological dimension. Then, of course, it will have to see itself as co-extensive with, and directly related to, the broad process of human liberation, because that is the stuff of which the anticipation of the kingdom is made. It will also have to be the critical ferment within this process, keeping an eye on the future and not allowing it to become set in ideologies legitimating privileges for the few — whoever they may be. It will have to resist the temptation to let itself be used as an instrument by those who try to identify the kingdom with "local approximations", or particular historical manifestations, thus halting the process. One basic point in its approach will have to be a dialectical understanding of the historical process itself, acquired through stressing its political dimension.

10. The choice for the Church in the 1970s

The process of liberation as it is going on now implies the need for the Church to make a choice. In a general and basic sort of way, Vatican II taught the Church that it cannot find its *raison d'être* in itself. It has to make definite acts of witness in relation to the process of liberation. In the light of its own sociological reality, the notion of its unity will tend to be conflictive.

Since it is in the world, and not merely facing the world, it will always be embodied in socio-cultural situations tied to historical projects. It will not be able to escape from a political significance, and any attempt to find a non-political refuge in its "spiritual mission" will prove illusory. Its task will be that of "an institution of social criticism" (Metz) within, and if necessary against, the historical process. In the Latin American situation, this means that its choice will have to be for the needs of liberation. As Gutiérrez says: "The world in which the Christian community must live and celebrate its eschatological hope is the world of social revolution. Its mission must be defined in relation to this. It has no other alternative. The only way its message of love can be made credible to the people of Latin America is through a break with the unjust social order with which it is identified in a thousand conscious or unconscious ways and an open commitment to a new society.28

V. Elements of a more precise definition

The most likely line of evolution for the theology of liberation (which is already in evidence) is for it to follow the dictates of the increasing need for a theology stemming from the Latin American situation; that is, from the original historical circumstances we are facing. This will imply an ever-increasing attention to the data of the sociological and economic analyses needed to interpret our situation more basically, as well as growing attention to the facts of the political process.

Theology will have to take more and more account of the complexity of these data, because Christians committed to the struggle for liberation will probably diverge from one another in practice. This has already begun to happen in the last few years. Within this broad context, the expression "theology of liberation" is of only limited importance, though it will probably remain rich enough in meaning for some time, serving as a general model for a wide variety of Christian reflection on different problems. What will probably happen is that this widespread phenomenon of reflection on faith will concentrate more on hard theological thinking based on the demands of the Latin American situation, and that this basic thinking will remain known as "theology of liberation".

1. *A theology sensitive to the most urgent demands of history*

If one wanted to make out a list of the ten most urgent problems facing the world, it should surely not be beyond the wit of, say, an international theological congress to agree on them . . . World hunger, the armaments industry, theatres of war, a strategy for peace without the threat of armed intervention and economic reprisals, the artificial nature of many engineered crises, consideration for the minimum requirements of the Third World, and so on.

It might be a little difficult — in view of our normal tendency to use verbal smoke-screens to prevent ourselves from seeing problems — to agree on an exact formulation, but surely we could hope for at least five real priorities to emerge in some shape, even if not in order of priority?

But why indulge in this childish game? The misfortune is that it is only a game, and that in reality it might be very difficult to reach any sort of agreement on such a priority listing. And if theologians couldn't manage it, how would heads of State fare? And come to think of it, would theologians do any better? Think of them... Think of the churches... Is their continual analysis of secondary or non-problems elevated to the rank of matters of life or death really a good prognosis of their ability to decide what the major problems facing the world really are?

This sort of game is only an illustration of what it is like to live in a world in conflict. Real examples are not hard to find. Look at the history of institutions that actually have to tackle questions such as the minimum requirements, in sheer justice, of the countries of the Third World. Look at what happened at the UNCTAD Conference in New Delhi; at the IMF meeting in Washington (1970) after which a thoroughly non-progressive representative from one Latin American country told *Le Monde* that in fact they had been given no effective chance to speak.

Nevertheless, in the world today there is something like a convergence of all the voices of protest. Not on the part of the official Churches, although something is happening within them, even though slowly. The convergence occurs in "UFOs", unofficial organizations, groups of people, generally without any reins of power in their hands, who have seen the need for the liberation of man in the world today. In his *Essay on Liberation*, Herbert Marcuse, analyzing the emergence and growth of this "true dimension of the revolution: liberation", gave free rein to utopianism and imagined the arising of "a new sensibility" and "a biological basis for socialism".

This convergence of protests on the most urgent needs is real enough, though still weak, still a "prophecy from outside", from the sidelines, made by those thrown out of the system and by a few great charismatic figures, some of them atheists. The Christians of the oppressed countries have an opportunity to share in this prophetic cry of protest through their own historical experience. To cry out with the prophets of course implies risks — inside the Church too, tied as it is to the altar cloths in so many little ways. Prophecy, being an existential risk, will normally be made in action rather than in words.

All this will seem facile to theologians preoccupied with the scientific validity of their contribution to theology. No matter. What does matter is that the general level of sensitivity should be raised; that there should be more agonizing over new demands that we can never quite meet. That is the line followed by the theology of liberation: sensitive to the major demands of the process of liberation, it sensitizes them in its truth — a much-needed function, since insensibility to these, among Christians and theologians of the more solemn variety, is unfortunately a widespread phenomenon.

As an indication of the opportunity — and mission — facing the theologians of the Third World, I should like to quote from a letter from a friend of many Latin American theologians, Paulo Freire:

"Sometimes, although I am not a theologian, simply a fascinated amateur of theology, which in many ways seems to echo what I think is the line along which my pedagogy is developing, I get the impression that the Third World could become a source of inspiration for theological renewal, through its utopian and prophetic character as an emergent world. The developed countries are prevented from exercising any prophetic role by their nature as societies whose future lies in the maintenance of their present affluence. They are denied hope, menaced by their establishments, who are afraid of any future that might shake their position. Their philosophical and theological tendency is pessimistic, denying man as a being in the process of transformation. This is why, if one is going to think outside the normal channels in the developed countries — and there are those who do — one has to think oneself into the 'Third World' mentality.

"This, it seems to me, must be the basic task, the prime concern, of the theologians of the Third World: to be men of the Third World. To steep themselves in it, so that they can be men of the world — utopian, prophetic, *hoping* men of the world. But this means renouncing power structures and establishments which, in this world, represent the world of oppression. It means taking sides with the oppressed, with the 'wretched of the earth', in a gesture of genuine love, which is not the gesture of attempting an impossible conciliation between those who oppress, stifle, exploit and kill and those who are oppressed, stifled, exploited and threatened with death".

2.   A *"praxiology"* of liberating faith in the world

(a) "Praxiology"   The word does not matter much. What matters is what it is supposed to convey. The historical emptiness of traditional theological and ecclesiastical language — one of the most frequent topics in the current debate on the essentials of theology — is particularly in evidence when it is shown up by problems, such as that of liberation, that relate directly to historical practical experience. At the risk of over-simplification, here are some practical points on which the theology of liberation should concentrate if it is not to fall into the same emptiness.

The central importance of practice as the starting-point for the theology of liberation has already been sufficiently emphasized. This has led to a terminology in which the task of transforming the world is so intimately linked to interpretation of the world, that the latter is seen to be impossible without the former. Any logic that is not a practical logic is done away with. The verbal magic of the "efficacious word" has disappeared. Speaking the truth is no longer an acceptable substitute for doing the truth.

Reflection ceases to have a world of its own and becomes simply a critical function of action; its world and its truth are experience itself, and there is no more flight to a verbal world decked with ontological considerations that reflect man's inability to deal with the real problems. Interpretation and the language in which it is expressed become the humanizing dimension of the act of transforming the world.

What is new about this, one might ask, since reflection has always been understood as a service to action? In theory perhaps, it has, but not in practice. The basic structures of traditional theological language are not historical. Its constituent categories aim at establishing an absolute truth without any intrinsic connexion with practice, which is seen as something that comes later, as a consequent application of the "truth" that precedes reality.

"Truth" understood in this way possessed a world of its own, a world of thought reality, not of the reality that exists; the world of eternity, not of time. "Traditional ecclesiastical terminologies had their ultimate concern in eternity, God, and the salvation of one's soul. Their relationship with the world, with life, with history, was at worst negative and at best purely tangential" (Alves). The source of these terminologies was basically Greek philosophy; their general tenor was anti-biblical.

The crisis of this "theistic" language can be summed up in one basic point: it de-historicizes God and man. History is emptied of any ultimate concern. The historic event is reduced to a simple fact of nature and loses its human-divine charge. In the Bible, on the other hand, words have meaning only as the expression of a deed, and theory has meaning only as the expression of practice.

Events form the structural centre of this biblical language. Not the casual events of the world of nature, but the human events of history. The historic dimension of events dominates the biblical outlook to such an extent that, in this pre-technical world, even the facts of nature came to be taken as a point of spontaneous interaction between God and man, which would be impossible for us today. Language in the Bible is "a footnote to historical events" (Alves). Greek theism, on the other hand, created a whole ideological sphere of truth totally separated from the world of man.

"Liberation", with the historical associations that the term connotes, is necessarily linked to effective action. Not the effectiveness of sheer production or "achievement". Technology has narrowed the concept of effectiveness, depriving it of its ethical and political content and reducing it to a level of pragmatism and utility. The "producer society" or "achievement society" is at the same time the "consumer society": man's activity and man himself are reduced to units of production and consumption of *things*. The semantic basis of this impoverished notion of effectiveness lies in the technical operations of nature. Man's activity is de-politicized and de-historicized; it is no longer an historical process. For the theology of liberation, on the other hand, the basis is experience of the participation of committed Christians in the struggle for liberation, and when it defines itself as "critical reflection on action", it is in fact defining itself as "praxiology", which T. Kotarbinski defined as "the general theory of efficient action".[29]

(b) Practice and truth "Truth", writes Alves, "is the name given by the historical community to those actions which were, are, and will be effective for the liberation of man". This identification of the idea of truth with the notion of effective action may seem provocative, as it brings out the historical dimension of truth against any attempt to establish its content before verifying it ("doing truth"), but it is not difficult to demonstrate its fidelity to the Bible – to the Johannine concept of truth, for example. The concept of efficacy used is not just that of "productivity" in the technological, materialistic sense, which removes much of the potential ambiguity of this new language; but perhaps the statement still needs clarifying.

In a certain sense the new formulations are an "anti-language", since one of their purposes is to demonstrate their cultural break from an earlier way of speaking about truth. The insistence on historicity in this formulation is a means of expressing the urgency of recovering a dimension missing from the earlier language: that of practice.

If one asks whether the old theological understanding of truth intrinsically included its historical efficacy in practice, the answer, simplifying somewhat, has to be No. Truth existed "of itself", in a sort of kingdom of its own, and any account taken of its historical dimension was something subsequent to, and pretty well independent of, the establishment of the truth. Adherence to truth was an intellectual matter, based either on its logic or the authority behind it. Basically truth was something to be accepted or not, and the purely intellectual act of accepting it or not in no way affected its status as truth. There was a "world of truth", an untouchable sphere existing over and above the vicissitudes of its working out in history.

This is a fundamental point: this "heaven of truth" possessed an appearance of reality of its own, independent of human action in relation to it. Hence it also possessed an "attributed efficacy", which was substituted for real historical efficacy. Truth was something valid in itself, and once that was established, it could not be either validated or invalidated by historical validations or invalidations. These could easily be dismissed as "imperfect applications" proper to the human condition, with no power to affect the absolute permanence of truth in itself.

This concept lies at the root of all dogmatism and authoritarianism — truth defined *a priori*, independently of its verification in history —, and of reaction: an appeal to "absoute values" as a means of resisting any historical change. Hence the tremendous ideological importance of the dualistic concept: the ideal truth, truth in itself, is what matters, and a declaration of fidelity to this serves to cover the absence of any real truth on the historical plane. Dualism implies a contempt of man and his history, shifts the ethical axis to the plane of idealism and so sets the whole area of historical reality free to be manipulated by the powers that be. Dualism, in short, is a political ideology of "law and order" and the *status quo*. In this context, it could be extremely interesting to analyze the dualism proper to technocratic thought, and then to inquire into the structural roots of a certain basic affinity between it and certain ecclesiastical circles. Present examples might be the strange enthusiasm shown by large sectors of the Church in the affluent societies for futurology, or for the Pearson Report on the "second decade of development", whose spontaneous rejection by Latin America is highly significant.

(c) Efficacy and gratuitousness The insistence on efficacy in human historical terms as an essential ingredient in the concept of truth can lay us open to the charge of failing to take account of the gratuitousness that is the essence of love, of being calculating in our understanding.

In the first place, the notion of efficacy as an ingredient of truth in practice was carefully distinguished from the concept of sheer "productivity". Criteria for establishing whether or not this efficacy exists can never be purely quantitative.

Productivity is conceived as something entirely quantifiable, whereas the notion of the historical efficacy of human actions requires qualitative criteria. If we remember that these actions are historical to the extent that they change the world for the benefit of humanity, rather than just continuing its previous mode of existence, then what is meant by qualitative criteria may become clearer. They have to be indices of the way in which the world is changed into a more human place by the effective action of man. Add the insistence that this action has to point towards liberation, and it becomes even clearer that the criteria are those of qualitative improvements in the service of man.

Once this is understood, the criticism of calculating immediate results is no longer valid. Yet it must be admitted that there is a grave danger of pre-judgment in selecting qualitative criteria. Action, if one looks for short-term results, can easily degenerate into mere activism, and no one should be more aware of this danger than Christians. Often, action forced upon one for apparently reasonable motives can be dehumanizing in its personal consequences; that is an inevitable concomitant of the climate of repression and secrecy in which so many of us are forced to operate. For us in this Continent it is important not to forget that there are many Christians who have opted for radical liberating action, often in accordance with their deepest beliefs, and often with a consciousness of the limited symbolic value of what they are doing. Unfortunately in some cases they seem to have lost sight of the deeper human values and operate solely in accordance with ideological criteria.

On the other hand, there are those who have seen that the introduction of new and original forms of Christian presence in the world involves personal risks, and whose commitment whatever the consequences has brought not only economic but physical and psychological suffering. In Latin America today, there are some who have literally "become eunuchs for the sake of the kingdom".

If, then, the objection that immediate effectiveness is the object cannot be sustained, since we are talking about effectiveness in a total human sense; if, furthermore, this effectiveness cannot be quantified in "productive" terms, since it has to be qualitatively humanizing action, the question remains: If we are talking about the action of love, how do we establish the presense or absence of love in historical action? There is an old reply to this: love is characterized by gratuitousness (Cf 1 Cor. 13). But what is meant by gratuitousness?

The fact that gratuitousness is an authentic ingredient in true love is undeniable, but one has to be careful of the context in which it is used, since, as has happened with so many other Christian terms, gratuitousness can be etherealized or put to use in the service of a particular ideology. There is, for example, a certain Germanic "personalist" linguistic tradition which makes great use of words like "personal", "interpersonal", "intersubjective", "gratuitous", but hides an evasion of the conflictive social reality behind an "ideology of personal love".

This kind of thought is apparent in one book entitled *Christ died gratuitously*,[30] which shows a real lack of sensitivity to the harsh realism of the play of history. It demonstrates the alienating devices of those who try to reduce the historicity of faith to those "moments of gratuitousness" in which, supposedly, "one loves, without a thought for anything other than love". This romantic and a-historical ideology of gratuitousness, typical of affluent, one-dimensional societies, leaves the course of injustice in the world totally untouched and leads ultimately to a religion applicable only to leisure moments. To apply this sort of evasive gratuitousness to him who was condemned and put to death as a subversive rebel, stirring up trouble against the occupying powers, is a real blasphemy against the Son of Man.

Gratuitousness, therefore, cannot be equated with mere uselessness. While no one would be so disrespectful to himself as to deny that poetry, music, the look that says more than words, the outstretched hand that means much more, are real human needs, one has to remember that there is a whole linguistic tradition of interpersonal communication that has become contaminated by the ideology of evasion. There is today a whole new field of encounter and communication, which is not likely to be swallowed up in hallowed institutional structures.

To sum up: The gratuitousness of true love can co-exist

with a firm consciousness of the implications of strategy and tactics; not everything that seems to be a quest for efficiency and no more is that in effect, since it can be a new form of laying down one's life for one's friends. Perhaps we need a new model of what that can imply, related to the concept of humanity as our neighbour, rather than just individuals. What is the new structural dimension of love in the context of a socialized world? On the level of experience that is "relished" and at the same time indicative of the personal need to love and be loved, what can it mean to give one's life for one's friends seen as the embodiment of the broad sweep of historical actions? Surely we need a framework of references to which we can relate our concept of gratuitous love?

(d) Faith as practice The old debate between orthodoxy and orthopraxis should not really need opening up here once more. In its classic form, it seems to suffer from a concept of "theory" that is in need of revision, and this, it seems to me, can be provided by a careful reading of the New Testament: Mark 25 or the First Letter of John will suffice for a start. The most dangerous heresies for the Church have always been those of practice, when the formality of preserving the purity of a doctrine has been overlaid by its betrayal through overt connivance with forces of oppression.

Yet faith must be understood as basically its practice, its working out in history rather than the simple sense of "practising the faith". This is stressed more and more strongly by contemporary theology, though some of its interpretations, while marking an advance on the Vatican I general view of faith as intellectual assent to truths, still do not amount to a vigorous historical concept. The aspects emphasized over the last decades — faith as dialogue, as interpersonal relationship; faith as an existential whole; the attitude of hope in the act of faith, and so on — generally stop well short of what I understand by liberating historical action. They generally refer mostly to the private sphere, staying locked into the small world of self and personal relationships. Despite their relative vitality, they still don't incorporate the broad sweep of human history and its urgent challenges.

The private theologies were radically challenged with the advent of Metz's political theology and Moltmann's theology of hope. The theology of liberation insists even more on the strong historical basis of faith, including the notion of effective historical action in its very vision of what constitutes faith. Faith can only be historically "true" when it "becomes truth": when it is historically effective in the liberation of man. Hence the "truth" dimension of faith becomes closely linked to its ethical and political dimensions.

Obviously, other elements are still relatively important to a true faith: it cannot, for example, be merely an intellectual adherence to an abstract notion of Christ; it must involve a direct personal commitment to God in Christ. On the church level, narrow confessional fidelity is no longer enough. This aspect, touching as it does on the relationship between Christianity and the sociological realities of the institutional structure of the Church — always there, but always provisional — cannot be resolved except in the broad context of what the Church is called to be in a world such as ours.

The implications of this cannot be decided by simple legal and confessional criteria, once one has understood that the Church cannot be the reason for its own existence, that it is called essentially to the service of man, in relation to the kingdom that is anticipated in history. Generally speaking, the criteria the churches use for determining the existence of true faith are, on the institutional level, necessarily external and somewhat arbitrary. Even when they are not based on events peculiar to the past of a particular church, they tend to be conditioned by its present sociological structure. It would be unreasonable to expect institutions to possess the sort of universal flexibility needed to overcome this tendency, and their criteria tend to suffer from the institutional tendency to minimum effort and self-preservation.

If the theology of liberation is to be a more effective instrument of critical reflection on faith, its criteria have to be of a different order from those still operative in the institutional spheres of the Church. These new criteria have already been touched on, with emphasis on the "major fact" of Christian participation in the struggle for liberation. The important point is that they cannot be established in the abstract, without reference to the historical context that determines the priorities of each situation.

Theology is only just beginning to face up to the question of what the events that go to make up the process of liberation mean for it. So before it starts judging them — "What has theology to say about this?" — it has to learn to listen to them — "What has this to say to theology?". This is the significance of the proposition adopted at the Buenos Aires Conference, by which the theologians taking part agreed that they had to participate in the process of liberation in order to find the material on which their theological thinking should be based.

Twentieth-century Catholic theology has made considerable efforts to deepen what has been called the *analysis fidei*, the effort at overall interpretation of the complex, dialectical whole that we call faith. Yet these efforts are now seen to have two serious limitations: their abstract quality and their lack of any reference to a historical and social setting. They became a sort of vivisection of faith in the heart of the individual.

The result is that we still do not possess anything that might be called a satisfactory *analysis historica fidei*: understanding which is "historical" in the sense of referring to what is implied in the concept of liberating historical action: the accumulation of data concerning the main challenges facing the process of liberation, alternative courses of action, ideological and political options, and so on. Those who are wedded to a certain concept of purity in theology could well be shocked by this requirement. What, they might ask, has theology to do with such a mass of non-ideological data? The question needs answering.

In the context of the theology of liberation, the demand that theological reflection on faith should become critical reflection on historical practice, has to be understood in a very particular way. The ambivalent reality of man's historical activity must not be idealized. This requires a sustained effort to evaluate the whole process of motivation underlying political decision-making, to recognize the advances and retreats, the significance of actions and people, the relative intensity of moments of political decision, the processes of qualitative shift through which new human experiences emerge, the changing ground of social language and its frames of reference, and so on.

Theological reflection, in short, must take its place where any human process of self-understanding has to be — in the real course of historical events. That applies both to interventions on the international scale and to the detailed working out of political strategy and tactics on the basis of a particular situation. At any level, even that of the most remote and scholarly research, theological investigation must involve itself in the practical problems arising from the historical demands of liberation.

In the broad spectrum of Christian theology today sensitivity to the historical character of human questioning is hardly even beginning to show. It could be difficult even to achieve a common consensus on the analytical content of the word "under-development" at an international theological congress! While such basic disagreements persist, the continued debates on esoteric points of doctrine, such as the Vatican attack on the Dutch Catechism (*The New Catechism*, London and New York, 1967) for its conception of transubstantiation, have a real ideological significance, in that they serve to mask any discussion of really important problems.

To determine what is really important, we start with the supposition that the proper subject matter of theology is the complex totality of all aspects of human activity that can be critically understood. The "truth" of faith, its verification, its "becoming true" in history, all comprise the living totality of practice. The aspect of "in what concerns faith" cannot be separated from the rest.

Saying that theology must concern itself with all aspects, and not with one only, is not elevating it to the status of a super-science, or giving it licence to embrace (or swallow) all the other sciences. It is simply stating that it either abstracts itself into theological purism and performs an alienating function, useful to the powers that benefit from a "spiritual" and politically malleable faith, or it accepts the real implications of the doctrine of incarnation. There is no attack on the "autonomy of the temporal sphere" or of the other sciences, as long as such autonomy is not taken as an ideological pretext for de-politicization, as is happening at present in many areas of Church reform through the conciliar doctrine of the temporal sphere.

Once theology decides to take a keen interest in all the elements that go to make up the complex whole of human activity, it will not take it long to realize how unreal many of its earlier concerns have been, and how remote its language. The consequence of this will not be a sort of totalitarian theological take-over, but the humility of a practical theology, one that listens more and speaks less, but when it speaks, says relevant things capable of making a deep impression on the critical consciousness even of those who do not share its beliefs.

This continued insistence on the need for theology to face up to the overall reality of human activity may seem excessive, but the reason for it is that many theologians still do not accept it. Nevertheless, I remain convinced that what makes reflection theological is the critical light it can shed on practice through asking questions related to faith. But since its concern is not merely to safeguard the theological cradle of reflection, but to give a real service — to be good theology, in fact — and since good theology cannot be pure theology (because that leaves various aspects of human activity out of account), there is not much purpose in establishing exact lines of demarcation between what is and what is not theology. Even "political theology" seems to have been caught in the net of constant re-definitions of what it can and cannot be, always seeking new answers to increasingly refined objections, instead of trying to identify the ideological background of those who make the objections.

Once he has isolated the real concern of the meaning of human activity for faith, the theologian has no need to ask anyone's permission to examine the whole dialectical plurality of all aspects of human activity in history, because if he did not do this he would be back in the realm of abstract activities, and so back to "bad" theology. In doing so, however, he must show a proper humility and capacity for listening, if he is not to fall back into the old vice of considering himself entitled to the last word on all interpretative formulae, and then into the presumed omniscience so characteristic of the traditional categories of theology.

To sum up: The theology of liberation can only make a significant contribution when it takes the need for inter-discipline among the sciences seriously. Besides the distinctive criteria stemming from the specifically theological question of the meaning of practice for faith — and even to be able to decide how far these criteria are valid — theology needs a whole range of other criteria derived from other angles of vision or practice, and these can only be obtained through a joint inter-disciplinary approach. There comes a point, however, when the essence of human activity, and therefore its most basic liberating content, becomes inaccessible to scientific inquiry. There is a limit to all criteria of quantification and qualification, because what they are analyzing is the infinite variety of human activity itself.

In the last analysis, theology too shares in this limitation, and theology above all should be able to recognise this limitation on its analytical reach. This recognition has an important political consequence: the quest for the mysterious efficacy of love in the complexity of all aspects of human activity has to be pushed to its final consequences and kept under constant review. Understood in its radical historicity (avoiding any form that falls back on confining love to the private sphere), this quest for love in action is the basic root of the quest for the liberating political efficacy of human action.

From this it follows that love, a properly theological term, is indispensable in any political struggle for liberation. Not that it is possible to speak of love only in theological terms, for that would be to insult all humanistic endeavours that have no need of theology to embark on a course leading to the liberation of man, even though much of their terminology is but a translation of theological terms into ones appropriate to a secularized world. But there is a final culminating point that love can reach in the process of liberation, the capacity for wholeheartedly laying down one's life for one's brothers, which strikes at the centre of all human questions related to liberation, and which finds both its symbol and its reality in the cross of Christ.

All humanist-inspired attempts at liberation are sooner or later bound to ask themselves what sense there is in the finally radical act of dying for others. Many do so, and many others accept it as a possibility without feeling the need to "theologize" this decision. But what this decision really involves implies a still more radical question if it is to be taken in full human knowledge, with full realization of its historical significance. And this radical question is theological.

The theology of liberation, as an effective process of critical reflection on historical practice, will have to go back to the theology of the cross. It will also have to strip it of the alienating mystifications that have accrued to it. The most obvious of these would seem to be the "theory of satisfaction", pushed to the extreme of the scapegoat who died for those who project on to him their own cowardice and failure to rise to the challenge of their historical responsibilities; another is the theory of the "reconciler" who pacifies everything and tries to avoid any sort of conflict. It will have to give back to the man Jesus his full integrity as a human being, and give his death the historical and political meaning that in fact it possessed. From there it can start to unravel the real meaning behind the symbolism of the New Testament: a whole line of challenge that has not yet been properly understood.

In this way, opting for a process of critical reflection on the present and on what is significant in the past of Judaeo-Christianity in the light of the present challenge, particularly the radical implications of the death of Christ, the theology of liberation can become a permanent and indispensable critical adjunct to the struggle for liberation.

VI. Differences and similarities

Obviously there are strong similarities between the aspirations and aims of the theology of liberation and those of other movements apparent in the theology of the developed world in the past few years. There is no denying the influence they have had on the genesis of the theology of liberation in Latin America. On the other hand, they also showed Latin American theologians that the time had come to stop importing ready-made theologies from Europe or the United States and to start working out their own.

The basic similarities do not need elucidating at this point, since they are clear enough, and this section concentrates more on the differences. Without trying to be polemical on this point, it is perhaps worth quoting a Latin American colleague who described the socially progressive theologies of the affluent world as "prologues in search of courage", in distinction to his characterization of the new attitude of Latin American theologians as, "courage with primitive weapons".

The schools of theology that concern us here are: the theology of revolution, political theology, the theology of hope, and the theology of questioning. Bibliographical references have been kept to a minimum.

1. *The theology of revolution*

It has been said in Europe that Latin America originated and then exported the theology of revolution. This strikes me as an exaggeration; the very extension of writings on the subject, as well as their somewhat cathartic nature and involved theorizing, categorize it as far more typical of the affluent world than of Latin America.[31] It was at the Ecumenical Conference on the subject of "Church and society" held in Geneva in 1966 that the spokesmen for the "Third World" introduced the term "revolution" into theological debate, and the spate of articles by Latin American writers for whom revolutionary terminology held no taboo seems to have contributed to the growing wave of discussion on the subject in theological circles. But since then its development has become more and more "de-contextualized", and far more typical of Europe than of Latin America.

After the initial joy we felt at seeing others apparently take an interest in our affairs, we Latin Americans could not help feeling disillusioned at the abstract turn the debate was taking. Not only was very little written in Latin America on the specific theme of "theology of revolution", but interest in it decreased as the discussion in Europe became more and more theoretical. When European texts were reproduced in Latin American publications, it was generally as a cover for discussion of particular cases.

There would seem to be some projective phenomenon

at work when the Europeans attribute to us Latin Americans an attempt at filling the historical vacuum felt by Christians with the theology of revolution.[32] No one can deny that the need to restructure the mission of Christianity in terms of changing the world is acutely felt in Latin America, but perhaps we feel less useless and confined in this respect than those Christians who are locked in the one-dimensional consumer societies. In addition, constant harking back to the past, whose hold still perpetuates social rites from the Middle Ages and similar phenomena, is a European rather than a Latin American problem. German intellectuals in particular are prone to these traumas, some of which have become apparent in the debate on the theology of revolution; in the fact that the political implications of the Enlightenment have still not been realized and that until now revolutions have always been frustrated in the country that has produced most writing on the subject of revolution; and in the almost congenital tendency to order and obedience that reached its culmination in the Third Reich.

There is probably a need for compensation evident in much that we produce as well, but we still have a right to tell the Europeans to stop projecting their own contemporary needs on to us. It is not true that the use of revolutionary vocabulary in Latin America is largely a quest for theological justification for projected action. It was of the Germans that Lenin said that before assaulting a railway station, they would probably buy a platform ticket.

In contrast to what Karl Rahner and others seem to insinuate, Latin America has not tried to centre the whole of theology on the idea of revolution.[33] As for the short-circuit sometimes proposed between the reality of the strategy and tactics of the revolution and "positive" theology, as propounded for example in Lehmann's *God's Action in History*, I believe the matter has to be approached from a different point of view.

Talk of God's presence in the world, of divine providence, of Christ acting in history, of the Spirit operating in the world, and so on, is a commonplace in Church and theological language. The texts of Vatican II are full of it. In the past, and even in the post-conciliar present, this "epiphanic" language has often been used to justify the *status quo* by assuring it that God was on its side. But if we understand it correctly, the language of "God's action in history", particularly in Lehmann's social ethos, actually means the opposite of what it is taken so often to mean: the fixing of God at certain points in history. Its aim is rather to put before us a *pro*-voking God, one who calls us forward, one working on the frontiers of the future foreseen in challenges to the existing social order. This is a biblical interpretation, because it is the language of the prophets. We therefore have to divorce the notion of God from its annexation in order to justify the rigid institutionalism of the *status quo*.

A little linguistic analysis, through ranging of opposites, would show that in the traditional and popular concept the presence of God is connected with institutional nouns, whereas in the language of Lehmann and even of Schaull, it is linked with nouns describing movement and the process of change. Semantically, there is an enormous difference in the meaning attached to the presence of God depending on the context in which it is understood to happen; between God in the institutions of the *status quo*, localized contrary to the notion of transcendence and to the prohibition of graven images, and God in the revolution, which is not a local configuration but a process — even though there is a danger of its becoming an idolatrous "image".

Symptomatically, those whose position in the debate is theologically in favour of the epiphany of God in institutions, the reactionaries, are generally those who accuse the "mobilizers" of harbouring idolatrous images of God, whereas in fact the opposite is true: it is the latter who are destroying the golden calves and practising a much-needed iconoclasm.

What does need to be understood is the way in which Latin American writings, particularly of the more occasional sort, talk of God and Christ in the context of strategy and tactics. There is a constant danger that this can be seen as using theology as justification for particular courses of action, though that is not the intention. Mentioning God in the context of particular levels of action is a proper feature of the process language of practice, and is not the same as the attempt to fix him for ever in institutions. We are not trying to base our strategy, still less our tactics, on divine rights or orders. Generally speaking, Latin Americans are not trying to find theological justifications for action before feeling free to undertake the actions.

When they dare to mention God and Christ at this level — as the prophets did when they referred to particular events — they are not trying to imprison God in this one "place". On the contrary, their aim is to free him from the prisons of the *status quo*, which arrogated to itself the last word on what is meant by being human, being democratic, being free, showing respect to God, and so on. Again, they are trying to unblock fixed ideas.

If one takes an explicit theology of revolution as an attempt to:

(*a*)   define the revolution to come, what it will be and should be, on the basis of theological categories;

(*b*)   seek theoretical permission, a divine licence, a legitimating and sacralizing cloak for being revolutionaries;

(*c*)   use the theoretical instrument of theology to provide the concrete constituent elements of a revolutionary ideology;

(*d*)   further use the theology to provide the basis for a revolutionary strategy and the tactical steps composing it; then I think it necessary to approach such a theology in an extremely critical spirit. Theology cannot, in itself, provide the instruments for such a task, nor is it its job to do so. The many writings, particularly the European ones, on the subject of the theology of revolution, show the inadequacies of the usual categories of theology for tackling this range of questions. If theology is to be competent to tackle the whole question of revolution, even without assuming totalitarian pretensions, we need a "revolution in theology".

What is *not* understood as theology of revolution in Latin America is an attempt to elaborate a *theory* of revolution on the basis of theology. Not even a Camilo Torres produced a theological theory of revolution. What there is, and will continue to be, is a preoccupation with theoretical reflection on the demands of the historical moment and the implications of the fact of revolution in practice for liberating Christian faith. A theology that keeps pace with the revolutionary commitment of Christians and defines itself as critical reflection on their actions, has to concern itself with revolution: not to elevate itself to the rank of Professor of Revolution, but to assist in freeing the ideological brakes that keep some Christians tied, in the name of faith, to reactionary systems supporting the established order — and that is no mean task! It must also make an effective contribution to the permanent presence of a critical consciousness at the heart of the revolutionary process, observing the methodological conditions already analyzed.

Such an undertaking is of course completely unacceptable as theology to those who want to maintain the traditional "Christian attitude" as one of reaction. They will castigate it as a "theologization of revolution". But if theology can accompany revolution on the lines indicated as being its proper task, then "theology of revolution" is an acceptable name for it. The danger to understanding lies in the isolation of themes such as "revolution" and "violence" from their circumstantial context, as has been done in much European writing on the subject. The lack of social analysis in these texts is astonishing; without even an attempt being made to see whether under-development really should be looked on as a form of dependence, what interest can such writing have for Latin America, other than as pieces of byzantine quibbling?

The theology of liberation has arisen at least partly as a reaction to the realization that it is not possible to isolate sub-themes from their broader thematic context and from their content of definitely located social analysis. It is an all-embracing reaction against the errors of compartmentalized theology, but it has not generally shown that it must broaden the canvas in polemical terms, perceiving, perhaps instinctively, that some polemics are really not worth the trouble.

So the answer to the question of whether the theology of liberation is part of the theology of revolution really depends on how the latter is understood: if as an attempt at writing the theory of revolution without reference to its settings, as is the case in so much European writing, then certainly not; but if as a broader and at the same time more definite concern with the revolutionary process, then undoubtedly it is.

In other words, the theology of liberation seeks to be critical reflection on revolutionary action in both its overall aspects and its detailed circumstances, but is not interested in discussing revolution as an abstract entity.

2. Political theology

The political theology of J. B. Metz and, in a slightly different form, of Jürgen Moltmann, is designedly different from older forms of theologization of the *raison d'état* that used to be implied by the name. It was developed as a critical reaction against the general modern tendency to relegate faith to the private spiritual sphere, and places strong emphasis on the political dimension of faith, seeking to re-establish the Church as an "institution of social criticism", without meaning this to imply any ferocious political partisanship. Metz's more recent writings contain frequent allusions to what he calls the "dangerous memory", by which he means the importance of Christians taking the unsatisfied desires of the past (its frustrated drives for liberty, its ambitions thwarted in mid-stream, the "subversive content" of Christianity, in short) out of the walls of tradition and examining them afresh.

This new form of political theology has generally been favourably acclaimed in Latin America, but, as with the theology of revolution, there are points on which the theology of liberation differs in the direction of more practical application. In Europe the theme seems to have become enmeshed in a series of secondary considerations forced upon its protagonists by criticism. Through having to reply to critics not generally motivated by a burning desire for change in the world, it has become somewhat aggressive itself, and lost something of its original drive and emotive power.

From the start, its sociological content, as a basis for reflection, has been somewhat vague. It seems afraid to name the organs of oppression openly. On the more theoretical level, there seems to be a strange opposition between the repeated postulate that the relationship between theory and practice needs fundamental re-thinking, and Metz's contention that his political theology can lead to no direct connexion with practice, a task he assigns to "political ethics".

In this way he perpetuates the old distinction between the contribution of dogmatic theology and that of ethics, basically alien to the Latin American approach.

The first exponents of the theology of liberation defined it as a political theology, and insisted on this point, without trying to distinguish it in any polemical way from the rather vaguer European school. But Latin American conditions played an important part in its reflections from the beginning, and this meant detailed analysis of the situation. This in turn means that for us there can be no real political theology that does not use an analytical language, which then implies a choice of analytical instrument, a choice that is in itself an ethical decision and not just a neutral choice between one possible instrument and another. This leads us to a double concept of ideology: the negative side, which idealizes and legitimates the existing order; and the positive, which is an "ideology of struggle", an ideology expressing our ethical and political decision.

European theologians seem to find great difficulty in embracing this positive form of ideology as an indispensable tool in choosing an instrument of analysis. This constantly incapacitates them in their efforts to marry the data resulting from analysis with the references provided by faith. They go on re-stating conditions in which committed reflection is possible instead of applying it to particular cases in the confident knowledge that the inherent ideological risk is itself a critical element of a permanent nature that, allied to the need for constant revision imposed by ever-changing patterns of action, will enable them to work out their criteria. The constantly frustrated attempt to work out all their criteria before applying any of them to practical situations reveals a sort of instinctively positivist autism — a very un-dialectical cast of thought, resulting in a hopeless effort to quantify even their criteria of qualification.

In Latin America we do not seem to be so seized by the need to construct total certainties on theoretical bases. Despite the poverty of our resources, our thought is always committed to the transformation of present reality. This means that our writings are always open to revision in the light of lessons drawn from experience. We do not believe in the permanent existence of a separate sphere of truth, as distinct from the sphere of reality, a distinction that seems to be a vice of traditional theological ecclesiastical language, capable only of idealistic criticism and not of critical realism.

Another difference is certainly in our ways of understanding the primacy of the political sphere. For us, it really means that politics constitutes the most important element of human activity, whereas in European political theology the impression is often that politics is "also" an important dimension, something added on to the rest, not something for which "also" is insufficient, something that has to be expressed with an "always".

3. The theology of hope

The contribution of Moltmann and his followers deserves a positive welcome as one of the best movements in contemporary theology, particularly for its criticism of the "epiphanic" thought based on institutions. Moltmann has been bold in calling attention to the problems that beset Christians today, at least in general terms, but the same criticism can be applied to him to a degree: that he does not name essential elements openly in his critical analysis. It would seem almost as though for a European theologian to dare to use the word "imperialism", he had to review the whole of Lenin's theory of imperialism and all the sub-theories derived from it!

The theology of liberation is not so much a theology of "hope", used as an abstract noun, as of the historical articulations of action born of hope and generative of hope. It is directed toward what Ernst Bloch called "deeds that are not only symbols, but embodiments of hope". Moltmann, as we have seen earlier in our brief review of Alves, assigns the role of articulation of the struggle for liberation to the promises of God; the theology of liberation would place the struggle of the exodus itself at the centre. But there is not much point in asking disruptive questions — whether it is the promises that confer hope, or whether action mediates the promises, which are found in the struggle. These are dialectical poles of the same process of assimilating the meaning of the struggle for liberation: the defining pole (action) is the understanding pole (critical reflection); one cannot exist without the other.

Yet there is a danger of unreflective action, just as there is of inactive reflection.

Proclaiming a hope that does not articulate and motivate the actual stages in the struggle, but feeds on promises "already given", runs the risk of leaving man an inactive spectator. Hope-in-action gives a content of reality to the promises, whereas hope-in-action is not really hope, but just waiting. Hopes should be acted on, not merely contemplated or believed.

When the new reality that has to be won through hard struggle is anticipated in promises described as real — the constant temptation of Christian verbalism centred on preaching, the power of the word, and so on — the real dialectics of the hard road to liberation is destroyed, because an exaggerated stress on promises removes concentration from the conflict of the present moment. The world comes to be seen as already prepared, already redeemed, and institutions as systems naturally open to change, constantly renewing themselves through a reforming action which may be conceived as operating from outside the system but in fact operates basically within it.

When this happens, the future (the eschatological pole), anticipated as "already present" through the promise "already given", ceases to be capable of radically negating the present through judging it in its most constitutive structural elements. Criticism can bear only on secondary aspects, on the need for improvements, leaving the essentials of resistance to change; and opposition to the established order no longer appears as the original and originating ground of hope, which can only arise to the extent that this struggle is taken with radical and definite seriousness.

The God who guarantees the promises "already given" can also play an alienating role. He can cease to reveal himself as Yahweh — he who is with his people — and the perspectives of liberation cease to be seen in the effective outcome of the struggle of the exodus. Then the possibilities for liberation, instead of being seen as greater than man's fearful prognosis dares to predict, and greater than man's limited powers of action can accomplish alone, become an illusory projection of desires that never become commitment. God, instead of being seen as the "plus" of history and in history, comes to play the part of substitute, and to limit the horizons open, since his promises are already made.

The theology of liberation must criticize subtle forms of man's alienation through utopias that do not contain the means of bringing about what they promise. The tendency to messianism in Latin America is one of the most vigorous potential revolutionary and liberating forces in the people, and one still largely unexplored. But it is also a deeply ambiguous phenomenon, and one that needs to be studied with critical rigour, watching for signs of hope deteriorating into mere waiting, and effective expression of the struggle into mere myth. Yet the biblical concept of messianism, understood as the collective expression of the historical hope of a people on its way, can become one of the most important sources for a theology of liberation.

4. The theology of questioning

This is not in itself such a clearly defined current as the preceding ones, but rather a quest for a more rigorous approach to theological questioning, derived from confrontation between theology and the data of the secular sciences. Horst Bastian's excellent book [34] demonstrates the lack of content of many theological questions as well as their ideological effect of covering up real questions about the nature of man. In their present formulation, many theological investigations lack any contact with reality.

Different scientific disciplines can provide a series of analytical approaches that show up the ideological mists in which much theological investigation is wrapped. Bastian seeks to situate questions in time and place through a psychology, sociology, anthropology and politics of questioning. His approach seems to go beyond the usual perspectives of the "sociology of knowledge" because of the stress he lays on the ethical and political dimension to questioning. Through their ignorance of the social and political roots to their questions, exegesis and theology fall all too easily into naive and dangerously ideological positions, usually in the direction of lending ideological support to the interests of the establishment.

One of the characteristics of the type of Latin American

thought emerging today is its ability to throw suspicion and work out hypotheses on any sort of political activity. In view of the hidden nature of many forms of manipulation — secret military agreements, the powerful but always half-hidden pressure of the CIA — we have had to develop a sharp critical faculty, capable of radical mistrust, and of finding instruments of proof which are not public property, but still tremendously important. The same approach has to be taken to the traditional expressions of theology, to reveal their hidden political content and their naiveté, to awaken the Christian consciousness to critical realism in the real play of history. These are tasks in which the theology of liberation can make use of the techniques proposed by the theology of questioning.

VII. Particular problems

Finally, I offer some examples of the sort of problems the theology of liberation has to face, concentrating on those that relate to the specific position of the Church and its historical conditioning.

1. *Characteristics of the situation*

(a) The novelty of the "Third World" revolution Neither the "bourgeois" French Revolution, nor the "proletarian" Russian one can serve as models. The Third World revolution has to take place in the global context of victorious technology. It is not just a revolution against lack of material goods, but against the new alienations of man in the affluent societies. It is anti-imperialist and anti-technocratic and dissatisfied with the idea of development, whose rejection is an important element in Latin American thinking, with the concomitant danger of anti-technical emotionalism.

(b) The new primacy of politics Besides resistance to "technocratic development", other factors conditioning this "urgent time" and imposing the primacy of politics are: the particular vulnerability of social systems based on caste; still incomplete organizational systems; the threat of "liberalization"; the straits in which radical minorities the system cannot encompass find themselves. Awareness of the new

central importance of politics is one of the most basic components of the thinking of *avant-garde* groups in Latin America.

(c) The waning of sacral justifications Systems obliged to defend themselves with violence, thereby revealing their basic nature of "institutionalized violence", seem obliged spend the last cartridges of sacral justification. Hence their loud appeals to their mission as safeguards of liberty, of democracy, and even of "spiritual values" and the traditions of the "Christian West". This creates an extremely propitious moment for denouncing hidden sacralizations of the existing order, and gives the Church the opportunity of standing clearly apart from any rites designed to uphold the *status quo*. In some Latin American countries, this situation has become paradigmatic.

3. Blockages and release in the Latin American Church

(a) Christians between "reconciliation" and conflict
Love tends toward reconciliation, dialogue, unity: this is basic to the Christian viewpoint. But can "love" be the ideology of peace at any price? Has this in fact been the Christian position in practice? In many ways it would seem that it has. Many Christians are simply incapable of accepting conflict as a fact, and as for deepening existing contradictions so as to bring out their real nature, this would be unthinkable for most. Yet the Bible is full of this: conversion, whether individual or societal, implies assumption of conflict. We need to get rid of falsely conciliatory disfigurements of Christian thought and behaviour, and to release the rebel, negative and conflictive energies of love so as to see it in action as conflict in history; to design models of Christian love that are also models of liberating struggle.

Today it is not only the specific problem of "violence" that forces one to a realistic acceptance of the existence of conflict; many everyday pastoral situations do the same. But the situation is much more acute in Latin America, where the obvious urgency of the struggle for liberation does not leave many alternatives open to the Church, and where sometimes priorities have to be decided in relation to only one possible course of action. "To take the side of the poor is to choose some against others, the oppressed against the oppressors, the poor against the rich . . . one class against another. This is a choice that divides the Church and introduces the struggle into its very life. Because many of the rich, most of them in fact, are Christians".[35]

(b) Post-conciliar reform   Reformers, whether Christian or Communist, tend to undervalue real conflicts. Changes are invoked in proclamation, "believed" in utopian and ideological fashion, not won in the fight. "*A priori* certainties", whether theological or pseudo-scientific — the laws of history, and so on — are deeply ambivalent: they can as well be used as justification for leaving things as they are, as seen as positive pointers in the direction of liberation: particularly when peace at any price is the only criterion in social behaviour.

There is a certain structural similarity between Christian and Communist reformers today. The "Communist threat" is more from the Right than from the Left. Compare the programmes of those Latin American Communist parties that follow the Moscow line with recent publications of Christian reformist provenance, and their behaviour.

The biggest differences are not now those between pre-conciliar traditionalists and post-conciliar reformers, who are almost exclusively concerned with internal ecclesial and pastoral reform and tend to avoid politics; they are between those and Christians truly committed to the needs of the struggle for liberation.

(c) Farewell to euphoria   There was a post-Medellín euphoria following on the post-conciliar euphoria. Both have now vanished. The Council hardly touched the problems of the Third World. *Populorum Progressio* was a step forward, but it was not up to expectations. Medellín heralded the "hour for action", but it does not seem to have been heard in some sectors of the Church, which creates a new situation for the *avant-garde*. Tempted to cut themselves off by their radicalism, and end up in a left-wing ghetto, they are now threatened with expulsion from the sociological body of the Church. At the same time, as a minority, they have a vital ecclesial function in relation to the emergence of a Latin American Church conscious of its historical mission.

(d) Church unity? In what sense?   This is one of the

most burning topics for Latin American Christians today. At the hierarchical level there is undoubtedly a seeking for an abstract concept of unity that is often an ideological cover for real differences. The concepts of unity and pluralism both need re-examination, if we are to produce a unity including the extra-mural voice of prophecy. The *avant-garde* groups will probably have to work this concept out themselves, as the institutional Church tends to a uniform notion of unity, either reducing rebels to obedience or throwing them out.

(e) The real political power of the Church The situation varies considerably from one country to another, with Uruguay representing the secular extreme and Colombia the other. But the Church has power everywhere in Latin America. If it attempts to withdraw from politics it is sabotaged by its own sociological reality; it just can't do it. That means that priests are also in some sense political figures, however much they may dislike the fact.

In asking the Church to dissociate itself through clear words and actions from the existing power structures, I am not demanding that the hierarchy should become committed partisans overnight, but only that they should free themselves, in an historically realistic manner, from a role that legitimates the established order; then they will leave room for a real range of political options within the Church.

At present this freedom of choice does not exist, even where it is proclaimed verbally. In this context the phrase "left-ward shift of the Church" becomes very ambiguous. For some it indicates a hope for a massive commitment of the Church to opposition to oppressive regimes — for which I do not believe conditions really exist. For others it simply means real freedom of choice, and an end of condemnations of "left-wing" options, which are always specifically condemned while conservative ones are generally tolerated; if conservative ones are rebuked, it is in general terms, except where the prevailing powers are as rabidly right-wing as in Brazil, where even the conservative "Tradition, Family and Property" programme was condemned.

(f) "Left-wing Constantinism"? Some groups have been accused of this. Their reply is that this is not their aim; they are merely giving the Church its true political weight,

and taking due account of the political potential of certain aspects of "popular religiosity" linked to social aspirations; there can be no Constantinian privileges if their aims are met, since the process of liberation will put the Church as we know it in jeopardy.

One danger they have to avoid is that of populism. Populism talks a lot about "the people", provides them with symbols (generally people) who supposedly represent them, and aims to eliminate the distinction between the élite and the masses, since the leader "of the people" represents both. But what the people really need is an awareness of their situation as other than the élite; to become the agents of their own representation at all levels instead of handing this over to others, who usually manipulate this position for their own advantage.

(g) The people of God: who are the people? The ecclesiological concept of the people of God cannot be used effectively without appropriate critical analysis. But of course it is used thus, and the result is to empty the expression of historical substance. Once one understands the Church as being in the world and not over against the world, the expression cannot be used to denote such a narrow grouping as the Sunday eucharistic assembly.

In the broadest sense, the people is everyone, but while this is valid, it has no operational value for the theology of liberation.

In figurative terms, the people as a whole, particularly those removed from all participation in the decision-making processes, are the "objective accumulator" of the conflicts and contradictions in society; within this whole there will be certain "subjective condensers" of the popular consciousness with regard to existing contradictions. If analysis can single out those who emerge subjectively as "condensers" of the popular awareness, this will provide a basic element for answering the question, because the answer will have to come through these conducting-wires of the process of self-awareness in the people.

The Church has to sort out its pastoral priorities in relation to those elements in which the people are "condensed". Not even the Church can behave as though it were in direct contact with "the people" every time some mass of people is involved in or with it.

One relevant factor in any analysis will have to be the fact that over half the population of this Continent is under twenty years old. The young — and again who are their "condensers"? — are a fundamentally important element in any assessment of who the people are.

(h) Discontinuity of the "time of liberation" The Bible, as we know, has a notion of "intense" or "vital" time (*kairós*), of "hours of visitation", "days of salvation", and so on. Such times are obviously part of chronological time, but special. It would be interesting to see how different Christian groups in Latin America live the urgency of time, and how their different perception of the "hour at hand" conditions the steps of their commitment to liberation.

In the same way, the theology of liberation has to ask what degree of intensity it attributes to its time, whereas the Church in Latin America as a whole has to ask whether its historical embodiment has not always been in the totally homogeneous "continuous time" of the *status quo*. Is the Church capable of responding to the challenge even of an "historic time", let alone a "revolutionary time"?

With its search for "integral" humanity, in overall terms such as "integral development", "full liberation", instead of concentrating on priorities of deeds and aspects, and with its desire always to find the "ultimate meaning" of man and history, this type of Christianity tends to fall into a wholly continuous and homogeneous time ("always", "eternity"). It tends to avoid confrontation with the heterogeneous and discontinuous times that co-exist in reality. To some extent, this is responsible for the Church's a-historicism on the one hand, and its docility to the "dominant time" of the established order on the other. The dominant time is also generally a "time of domination" to the extent that it tends to lend homogeneity and permanence to what already exists; it is the time that perpetuates what is, the time of resistance to change. This accords with many basic "Christian" concepts; with their predilection (or at least predisposition) for escape from conflict in times of struggle — as can be seen in the ethical terms "peace", "order", "harmony", "reconciliation", and so on, and the doctrinal-juridical "tradition" or "respect for the values of" this or that institution . . .

3. · Fundamental theological gaps

Leaving aside basic problems of theological methodology (some of which have already been touched on in the course of this study), and of fundamental theology (such as revelation, the "signs of the times" and others), there are two fundamental gaps which are vital for the theology of liberation: they are *christological* and *hermeneutical*.

(a) The need for a Latin American christology What does Christ mean for the process of liberation in Latin America? On the one hand there is the vague, general christology *ad usum omnium*, unrelated to any particular situation, and on the other, particular embodiments designed to fit a particular ideological purpose at a particular moment. Somewhere between the two there is a legitimate need for a historically mediating christology relevant to the basic problems of a given historical situation.

The second Vatican council oscillated between a still basically "ecclesiastical" christology, in the almost purely sociological and institutional sense (Christ made present in *this* liturgy, *this* form of celebrating the eucharist, mediated through *this* historical configuration of the Church), and one of "Christ acting in the world", sketched in the vaguest terms but still basically ambiguous in its categories. "The presence of the risen Christ in the world", "Christ the alpha and omega", and similar phrases, are not only of little use to a liberating evangelization in a world torn by conflict, but can too easily be used in a mainly "epiphanic" sense: He is said to act through institutions, and thus justifies their existence.

What is surprising is the lack of any sense of crisis about the meaning of Christ in the very midst of an acute crisis about the meaning of the Church. That doesn't mean that Christ is not important in the current crisis of faith in Latin America, but he is certainly not such an intensely-felt part of it as the Church. One possibility is that the Christ most generally recognized is so vague and distant a figure that he remains basically likeable and liked, despite the violent confrontations between the vanguard of liberation and "his"

Church. Such a distant Christ can hardly make much impact.

On the other hand there are "christological mediations" which, though they have at least the merit of being definite, still distort the image. These are the symbolic representations of Christ based on Camilo Torres, Che Guevara and other similar symbolic figures.

There is, then, a lack of relevant yet authentic Christology, and a need for one.

(b) Hermeneutics and practice Contemporary philosophy has shifted the hermeneutical problem of "ancient texts" towards confrontation with present historical reality. The original "text" has become our reality and our practice. Meanwhile the exegetes continue to work out a "biblical hermeneutics" without being much disturbed by any consideration of the data offered by the secular sciences or practical needs. The close relationship between their political naiveté, sometimes outright reaction, and their "hermeneutical principles" (and their concept of "revelation") comprises a chapter in the history of ideology which has still to be written. It is as though Christianity itself appeared to us as an unknown past to which we had to have a hermeneutical key before we could understand it. I suspect that we don't have the key precisely because so much of the Church's sociological past is an obstacle to understanding.

We need to reject a "fundamentalism of the Left" composed of short-circuits: attempts to transplant biblical paradigms and situations into our world without understanding their historical circumstances. It is equally false to state that the whole biblical framework, with its infinite variety of paradigms and situations, is an adequate basis for establishing a satisfactory complex dialectics of hermeneutical principles.

The theology of liberation sees itself as critical reflection on present historical practice in all its intensity and complexity. Its "text" is our situation, and our situation is our primary and basic reference point. The others — the Bible, tradition, the magisterium or teaching authority of the Church, history of dogma, and so on — even though they need to be worked out in contemporary practice, do not constitute a primary source of "truth in itself" unconnected with the historical "now" of truth-in-action.

The main problem for us is that of hermeneutical criteria. The usual views of exegetes who "work on the sacred text" are of little use to us, because we want to "work on the reality of today". Inoculated against facile concordances, we are no longer interested in generic considerations like the differences between biblical and Greek thought (I should add that we are just as suspicious of the criteria used by the secular sciences, which can too easily hide ideological prejudices).

What then are we left with? With the inescapable importance of the ethical leap, the political choice, contained in any attempt at interpreting a historical situation. We can no longer believe in the possibility of establishing truth in a sphere of its own, independent of the sphere of historical reality. Since the roads leading to the meaning of the historical experiences in the past of Judaeo-Christianity are largely blocked by ideologies (because the criteria governing the means of access themselves need freeing from their ideological domination), where do we go from here?

I suspect there is no other way than through the process of liberating our criteria, including those governing the ethical and political choice that decides our personal commitment. We have to produce essays in criticism that we test constantly against experiments in practice. Gradually we have to bring together interpretations of present-day reality and a discovery of relevant criteria in the history of Judaeo-Christianity. But all this has to take place in the "pressing time" of the needs of the process of liberation, which cannot be postponed. We can't wait. In the words of a Brazilian protest song, we are "in a day of war, which is a day without sun".

NOTES

1   An extended version of a report written at the request of the Latin American secretariat of the International Movement of Catholic Students (MIEC).

2   For instance: A. Gheerbrant, *L'église rebelle d'Amérique latine* (Paris, 1969); G. Vaccari (ed.), *Teologia della rivoluzione* (Milan, 1969).
3   For instance: J. Comblin, *Teologia do desenvolvimento* (Belo Horizonte, 1968); id., *Christianismo y desarollo* (Quito, 1970); François Houtart, *Eleventh Hour: Explosion of a Church* (London, 1967); H. Assmann, "Tarefas e limitacões de uma teologia do desenvolvimento", in *Vozes* 62 (1968); René Laurentin, *Développement et salut* (Paris, 1969); G. Bauer, *Towards a Theology of Development* (Geneva, 1970).
4   For further discussion of this point, see my chapter, "Theologie der Revolution als Sprach-Ikonoklasmus und neues Sprechen" in Feil & Weth, *op. cit.*
5   R. Certulo, "Teoría y práctica de la política de desarollo de la iglesia", in *Perspectivas de Diálogo* 46 (1970).
6   Cf. A. Aguilar & others (eds.), *Desarollismo y desarollo* (Buenos Aires, 1969), especially pp. 1-100, which are a refutation of various theories on the under-development of Latin America.
7   Referred to henceforth as I and II. I, *Liberación, opción de la iglesia en la decada del 70*, contains, *inter al.*, chapters by Gustavo Gutiérrez; II, *Aportes para la liberación*, contains, *inter al.*, a chapter by J. A. Hernándes, "Outline of a Theology of Liberation" (both Bogotá, 1970). (Cf also *Christians and Socialism*, ed. Eagleson [New York, 1975]).
8   E. Pironio, "Teología de la liberación", in *Teología* 8 (Buenos Aires, 1970). This article is important, both as an expression of the basic ideas put forward by the theology of liberation, and an illustration of the fears felt about it at hierarchical level.
9   Gutiérrez in I, p. 26.
10 Pérz in II, p. 4.
11 Gutiérrez in I, p. 17.
12 Hernández in II, p. 37.
13 Gutiérrez in I, p. 36.
14 *Ibid.*
15 II, Intro., and Pérez in II, p. 4.
16 Gustavo Gutiérrez, *A Theology of Liberation* (New York, 1973), pp. 3-20.
17 Gutiérrez in I, p. 27ff; Hernández in II, p. 39ff. Harvey Cox has made an interesting admission on this point: "I should first of all declare that I have recently been very much influenced by certain theological currents from Latin America, especially by the description of theology given by Gustavo Gutiérrez of Peru, who says that theology is a science in the course of development and that its very definition changes in the course of this development . . ." in *Víspera* 19-20 (1970), p. 51.
18 J. L. Segundo, *De la sociedad a la teología* (Buenos Aires, 1970). Here each theological chapter is preceded by a sociological examination

of the same subject-matter.

19   Gutiérrez in I, p. 25. E. Pironio also takes what he calls "the event" as the starting point for his reflections, but adds to "the growing commitment of particular groups (the young, for example), and the approach adopted by the Latin American Church at Medellín", the other aspect of "the speechless clamour rising from millions, beseeching their pastors for a *liberation* that is not coming to them from any other source".

20   Harvey Cox again makes the same point: "Theology in the first instance should not be a systematic or speculative discipline, but a critical one, and to that end should work more and more with the tools of the social sciences rather than with the traditional categories of philosophy". *Art. cit.*, p. 51.

21   On this point, Giulio Girardi writes: "The Council ended with the decree on the Church in the world today, in a climate of dialogue, of reconciliation, almost of idyll ... But the idyll did not last long. The Church and the world soon showed themselves to be two fairly incompatible characters, and a divorce would seem to be in the offing. The spell broke almost as soon as the explosive content of the approach was realized. In facing the problems of the world, the Church had to take stock of its own social system, and many Christians felt the need to call it radically into question. Then the Church realized that calling the system into question was calling itself into question ... The approach to the world that started as a gesture of reconciliation has become a declaration of war". *Amour Chrétien et conflit de classes* (Paris, 1970), pp. 81-2. This touches on the point that most distinguishes the *avant-garde* Christians of the Third World from those of the affluent nations.

22   J. L. Segundo, in a duplicated article.

23   R. Certulo, in *Perspectivas de Diálogo* 46 (1972), p. 182.

24   R. Alves, *El Pueblo de Dios y la liberación del hombre*, ISAL docs. 3 (1970), p. 9ff.

25   Gutiérrez in I, p. 48.

26   *Ibid.*, I, p. 51. Gutiérrez takes up a theme common to many contemporary theologians, but radicalizes its implications: "There are not two histories, one profane and one sacred, 'joined together' or 'closely linked' but one process of human becoming taken on irreversibly by Christ, the Lord of history". "It is not enough to say that love of God is inseparable from love of one's neighbour. We have to say that love of God is inescapably expressed in love of one's neighbour". I, pp. 48, 52.

27   *Ibid.*, I, p. 49.

28   *Ibid.*, I, p. 56.

29   T. Kotarbinski, *Praxiology: an Introduction to the Sciences of Efficient Action* (Oxford, 1965).

30   G. Mainberger, *Jesus starb umsonst. Sätze die wir noch glauben können* (Freiburg im Breisgau, 1970), pp. 79ff.
31   Cf. the full bibliography in E. Feil & R. Weth, *op. cit.*
32   Karl Rahner appears to insinuate this in a still unpublished text prepared at the request of the Vatican: "Theses quaedam de 'theologia revolutionis' quas subcommissioni cuidam Pontificae Commissionis Theologiae proponit Carolus Rahner" (I quote from a photocopy of the original typescript). He repeats the idea of the *defectus functionis* which leads Latin American Christians to identify with the revolutionary cause. But he does admit the revolutionary situation as not only a determinant in the Third World, but universal today, and defends a "theology of revolution" understood as an integral part of pastoral theology.
33   Rahner, *op. cit.*, p. 4: ". . . tamquam unicus clavis et principium totius theologiae, ut hodie non pauci sentiunt".
34   H. D. Bastian, *Theologie der Frage* (Munich, 1969).
35   G. Girardi, *Amour chrétien et conflit de classes, op. cit.*, pp. 82-3.

III Liberation:
the implications of a new theological language

III Liberation: the implications of a new theological language

THIS chapter is based on the proceedings of two theological conferences.[1] These meetings tried to assess the need for a social, economic and political instrument of analysis capable of reflecting on faith as the historical embodiment of love. As a result the conferences called for a theory of revolution, which they declared was necessary before theological reflection could begin. This was something quite new in theology.

The next stage was the appearance of works by Gustavo Gutiérrez and Pablo Richard.[2] By now the very ubiquitousness of the "language of liberation" put it in danger of being swallowed up by the ecclesiastical machine. This led many people to want to abandon the term "theology of liberation" in favour of the circumlocution "theological reflection in a context of liberation". What had happened in so short a time to the theological matter of Vatican II — used as the final adaptation of progressive, liberal thought, and so as a barrier to revolutionary expectations in Latin America — was endangering at least the more popular forms of the "theology of liberation".

We must go back to the essentials, and stress what distinguishes theological reflection in Latin America from that of the affluent nations. This, to my mind, lies in the fact that we have assimilated — somewhat confusedly, maybe, but still characteristically and effectively — three levels of approach necessary for historical reflection on faith as the practice of liberation. If theological reflection is to be historically and practically valid, then it has to operate on these three levels, which are:

1. *The level of social, economic and political analysis*; the level, that is, of an attempt at rational interpretation of the reality of history — which in itself implies an ethical and political decision in the very selection of the instruments of analysis, since these can never be completely neutral.

2. *The level of opting for particular political theories and approaches*. These could be "imposed" by the results of the initial work of analysis, but their choice is also determined by an ethical element not derived from the analysis itself: man's capacity for making himself responsible for history.

3. *The level of strategy and tactics*. The general political theories require planned implementation, and this implies obedience and discipline — to borrow traditional terms — within an effective form of political action.

The complexity of the implications at each of these levels, and the risks inherent in a theological approach that deliberately embraces the practical aspects of the much-quoted historicity of faith and reflection on it, are obvious. But is there another less "ideological" approach — or are we right in claiming that we have abundantly proved to ourselves that all others are inevitably more ideological and ultimately idealistic rather than realistic? The classical temptation of theology has been to adopt a global viewpoint to the exclusion of a historicity that may be partial, but is at least definite and real. Hence the privilege it has always accorded to philosophy at the expense of the practical sciences. This temptation can be seen at work again today, in belated and ingenuous flirtations with philosophies whose ideological content is not difficult to unmask. The social teaching of the Church, for example, has been imprisoned in the presumedly philosophical tenets of Western humanism, with tragic results for its attempts at reform.

On the other hand, the secular sciences such as economics and sociology are themselves in a state of crisis, and need to be used critically, with an approach rooted in ethical and political considerations, themselves based ultimately on radically new humanist thought. If this criticism is going to become genuinely philosophical and theological, it will probably have to oppose the "humanist" philosophies now current. The new humanist efforts are already "anti-humanist" in the sense of being opposed to the traditional Western humanism.

Under the pressures of the historical needs of the Continent, certain sectors of Latin American Christianity seem to have decided that a real encounter with the radical imperatives of faith — which are also in some senses those of philosophy — means tackling them on the three levels at once. That does not imply a rejection of philosophy as such, but a recognition of the processes necessary for philosophical thought. On the theological plane, it certainly implies an abandonment of the traditional methods of theology in affluent societies. One might say that a constant juggling with "the conditions under which it might be possible to act courageously" has been replaced by "courage in practice with primitive weapons": and for one simple reason: that in the end history will judge us by how much we have loved.

I. Sociological and ideological implications of the language of liberation

I have already touched on the extraordinary diffusion of the language of liberation throughout Latin America, with the concomitant danger that its very popularity will dissipate its meaning, a danger that increases as the language of liberation is taken up in official ecclesiastical circles to fill the void left by the obvious bankruptcy of traditional church language. We must recall the original implications of this language, particularly of its references to elements of social analysis and ethical and political decision, which lie at the heart of its basic semantics.

We are dealing with something virtually unknown in contemporary theology. Whereas all theology has a conscious or latent ideological stance, the theology of liberation, through its adoption of the "language of liberation", bases its reflection directly on a particular form of social analysis, recognizing and deliberately adopting the ideological position this implies. This is a completely new departure, and entails important methodological implications.

1. Liberation as a new historical consciousness

The language of liberation enshrines a specifically new historical consciousness: it shows our realization of the fact that our real historical situation is one of dominated peoples. It is an act of rebellious presence in an historical context of slavery and domination. As such it implies more of a break with the past than a desire for continuity.

This new language is the factual expression of a new state of consciousness with particular revolutionary implications. Given its present speed and extension, it is difficult to find any parallel in church history in Latin America — or elsewhere. In Latin America, not even the emancipatory ideals of the first wave of independence spread so far and so fast, or acted as such a general magnet. Liberation, the second and true wave of independence for our countries, places us in largely uncharted revolutionary waters.

There are of course other revolutionary currents abroad in the world: the oft-quoted "youth power", the dissident minorities in the colonial nations, a certain degree of revolt among the intelligentsia, and so on. Although they have points of resemblance, none of these currents really coincides in analysis or aims with the process of liberation. The real starting-point for a "Latin American theology of liberation" has to be found elsewhere,[3] in our specific struggle for liberation from our situation as dominated peoples.

A fitting task for theology, within the context of a Christian preaching of the all-embracing nature of charity, would be to fill the concept of liberation with meaning for the whole person. Gutiérrez's definition of the three levels is entirely appropriate in this context for a theological approach to liberation: "(i) Political liberation of socially oppressed peoples and classes; (ii) liberation of man throughout the course of history; and (iii) liberation from sin, the root of all evil, in preparation for a life of communion of all mankind in the Lord". It is equally appropriate for theology to seek other extensions of the concept of liberation, but it would be an extreme disservice to empty the process of liberation of the specific revolutionary implications that are at the root of its language and the reason for its diffusion.

2. Sociological elements necessary to this new historical consciousness

There are two basic and related facts underlying the growth of the language of liberation:

(*a*) The failure of the reform and development options with their palliative tactics for the creation of a new form of society. As long as the structural basics remain the same, the dynamics of the crisis will continue to require more radical solutions. Even though some reforms produce changes that are then seen to be irreversible, these tend to create greater incongruities in the future.

(*b*) A realization of the mechanics of exploitation and domination, whether from within the country or from outside, brings a better understanding of the implications and consequences of the imperialism and nationalism that have shaped much of our history. This realization leads to the formation of subversive groups on one side and repressive practices on the other.

Since the beginning of the 1960s, the social sciences in Latin America have come to concentrate on the theme of dependence, which has become a scientific category used to describe the state in which the nations of Latin America exist. This is an innovation, or rather a break with their past, in subject matter and in methodology.

The theory of dependence is still evolving, correcting earlier errors of focus as it does, but a series of recent works has given it a definite status by placing it at the centre of academic discussion on development. The earlier errors of focus have been corrected by understanding two main points above all: firstly, that dependence is not merely an external factor, and to see it as such risks falling into the comfortable posture of ignoring the internal dynamism of all sorts of agencies of oppression that go to make up the structural reality of our countries: dependence must be seen as an overall conditioning factor in our history, moulding us into what we have become culturally, socially, economically and politically; secondly, that "although dependence is part of the global picture of imperialist theory, it should also contribute to its reformulation".[3]

The concept of dependence springs from the basic failure of development models. Its adoption by the social sciences represents a break with the past, in which they tended to serve as ideological vehicles for these models. There is no further attempt to correct or build on the concept of development; it is now rejected and we have entered the phase of open opposition to it.

3. Liberation as the political correlative of dependence

The language of liberation is essentially no more than the political correlative of the sociological language of the analysis of dependence, though too rigid a separation between the two should clearly not be made. The decisive crossroads in the history of the social sciences is reflected in a corresponding "Latin American political science at the crossroads".[4] The basic themes — dependence, exploitation, imperialism, violence, power, liberation, and so on — always have a political dimension as an intrinsic component. Hence the need for an inter-disciplinary approach, a bringing of all the disciplines to bear on the central problem.

The notion of "crisis", long current in sociology, takes on a new meaning when its political implications have been fully understood. In the Latin American context, the "crisis" of society has been defined as a situation in which a society or nation has been led by its historical development to a point where its contradictions and incongruities are such that they cannot be resolved without producing basic changes leading to a new type of social order.

The language of liberation came into being through a realization of the consequences, in terms of political struggle, of our situation as dominated peoples. Semantically, it depends on the sociological analysis already referred to. One of its basic implications is therefore the rejection of the development option in whatever guise it shows itself, and it is above all a means of defining the strategy and tactics of the struggle for liberation, the revolutionary option that must lead to an historical outlook opposed to the *status quo*.

For most of those who use this language, this implies the use of a sociological analysis derived from Marxism, and a strategy that will lead to a form of socialist society. On this still somewhat abstract level, the implications are of an increasingly open confrontation with imperialism, although the priorities in terms of method and tactics may still have to be worked out.

4. The danger of vacuity

There is a close correlation between the various phases in the origin and diffusion of the language of liberation and the understanding by large sections of the Christians of Latin America of the sociological analysis of the situation of dependence and its political implications. This correlation means that the language is being more deeply understood, but it also means that it is in danger of losing its real meaning.

We have already touched on the negative side: that the rapid diffusion of this language, and its adoption in official church circles, could mean that its real origin will be forgotten. This is not as a spontaneous development within the current of post-conciliar reform, but as something extraneous to the churches, an immigrant language from outside. The churches of Latin America are in fact largely lacking in any theology consistent with the historic challenge facing them. This theological vacuum is even more evident among those groups of Christians who have realized the inadequacy of the theology, or theologies, of the second Vatican council, and even of the most progressive theologies of the affluent societies, in the context of the specific problems of Latin America.

That could explain a major element of the almost desperate recourse to the language of liberation, which has been used to fill in where the traditional language of the Church is no longer adequate, without any clear appreciation of the historical demands implicit in its use. This can perhaps be seen in the new jargon of groups whose intentions in regard to church matters stop short at reform, and who talk of a liberating liturgy, a liberating catechesis, and so forth. Even if such a phenomenon may represent some vague form of support for the process of liberation, it is still a misuse of a language forged to be historically contentious — an articulation of the true struggle for the liberation of our countries.

On the positive side, there is a growing use of the language of liberation by many front-line Christian groups, determined to pursue its use to the final practical implications. But these groups remain prophetic minorities, with no links with the institutional Church. While it may not be difficult to find an ecclesial role for them theologically, in terms of a Church for the world, the reality is sociologically very different: it is in fact considered "normal" for the institution to reject these groups, or at least push them to one side.

The theology of liberation is then faced with the same problems as confront those social scientists bent on "a new, subversive, rebel, guerrilla and political science". The problem consists in "picking out the key groups that ought to be served by science and in identifying with them, thereby making them reference points for the scientist, who would pursue his investigations with them in mind".[5] I do not see how a similar process of choosing sides can be avoided in the present climate of Latin American Christianity. This must not exclude the quest for the fulness of love and service in practice and not merely in intention: nor should we forget that this very service implies taking sides with the struggle for liberation and those committed to it. That means recognizing the class struggle within the bosom of the Church — acknowledging it, not starting it, because it already plays a part in the social framework of the churches. Finally, we must recognize that this "minority theology" — which is so precisely because it needs to remain flexible enough to tackle all the problems of our dominated peoples — is even more of a minority movement when set in a world-wide Christian context. Those who have any knowledge of the "best" in the theology of the affluent societies will know that conditions are hardly ripe for our view of the phenomenon of underdevelopment as a form of dependence to cut much ice in an international theological congress. It would be impossible to try to persuade such a gathering that a basic pre-condition of dialogue was the rejection of the idea of development as it is understood in Latin America. All the evidence is that outside bodies, theological or other, still lack a basic understanding of the essential elements of the problems of liberation.

The theology of liberation has to stand largely on its own, and the challenge it faces is not to defraud those who expect it to be what it originally set out to be — critical and motivating reflection on faith as the historical embodiment of liberation — by falling back on vague verbal flirtation with the idea of liberation.

II. Can strategy and tactics be subjects for theology?

There is a growing demand, particularly from those Christian groups most closely involved in the struggle for liberation, for a closer link between reflection on ideology and politics and reflection on faith. This demand springs from their experience that vague "evangelical motives" (such as those proposed by Catholic Action, or found in the social teaching of the Church) are insufficient to secure commitment, through being too much of a preamble to action and finally leaving the militant on his own when it comes to the most difficult part: trying to put principles into practice. They are too distant from reality, speaking of commitment in a language far removed from the level of strategy and tactics, which for many means that they are not in fact speaking of commitment in any sense that they can call real.

On the other hand, there is the received doctrine that theology as it is known does not possess "sources" (the Bible, tradition, the magisterium, doctrinal history) that provide "theological" resources for coming down to the level of strategy and tactics and playing a directly supportive role in the formulation of political and economic projects.

There is a good reason for this: a desire to avoid falling back into the trap of reactionary "political theologies" — theologies that legitimate and sacralize the *status quo*. The same applies even if the *status quo* is a new one resulting from a victorious revolution. This desire has become a dominant feature of current European discussion on the subject — it would be unkind to call it a pretext for non-involvement. It is also supported by the conciliar doctrine of the "autonomy of the temporal sphere", and by "secularization theology".

All this produces a picture full of contradictions and ambiguities. Karl Rahner, for instance, states that there cannot, nor should there, exist a "theology of revolution" as such, but there can exist something like a "pastoral theology of revolution" that can make forays into the arena of strategy and tactics. Metz relegates the task of defining practical demands to "political ethics", reserving for "political theology" the somewhat vague role of a theological hermeneutics for political ethics, which — in my view — not only perpetuates the old dichotomy between dogma and morals in a new form, but also fails to resolve the problem of the failure of generic criteria of "Christian inspiration" in obtaining commitment. The higher reaches of the ecclesiastical hierarchy avoid the pitfalls of considering how faith can be worked out in practice by jumping clean over them and assuming that the question has already been answered. Symptomatic of this is the repeated insistence, in documents like *Populorum progressio*, that the "specific contribution" of Christianity consists in providing a "global", "integral" view of man and history.

One relatively easy way out of the dilemma is to insist on the primacy of the "prophetic" element in theological endeavour. This should not be denied, but it can easily lead to leaving everything else on one side and opting for a form of reflection on faith that approximates as closely as possible to the ambiguities of practice, with the result that a whole series of methodological innovations are allowed in practice, while theology remains on a separate plane, obeying a different set of rules, and lacking the time or the interest to consider the question of whether each and every theology must have a social setting, the question of the necessary historicity of theological thinking. But only after consideration of these questions can we draw the methodological consequences appropriate to each level of reflection on faith.

One is forced to the conclusion that the theology of the affluent societies has armed itself with an adequate battery of subterfuges and excuses in order to avoid facing this kind of question. Even its most *avant-garde* schools, socially speaking, set limits to their own spheres of competence, and decide where they can and cannot intervene. The theology of affluence has created a sea of calm around itself, in which it can sit back and flirt at a distance with the idea of revolution, but without getting its own hands dirty in the process. It would be good to see the theologians of the affluent societies take on the task of finally freeing theology from its last traces of idealism, of explaining the methodological implications of the fact that theology is always rooted in a particular social setting, and of making definite attempts at establishing bases for a real connexion between the classical sources of theology and the primordial *locus theologicus* represented by man's historical experience in the present.

1. Theology has always a social setting

There never has been, nor is there now, such a thing as a theology outside time, disconnected from any historical conditioning, whether manifest or hidden. All theology is necessarily historical in the sense that it has a social setting and, consequently, a discernible ideological undercurrent. In view of this it is strange that many theologians of the affluent societies, while they recognize this fact in a general way, fail to appreciate the consequences of the setting of their theology and persist in the idealist temptation of political abstention. They seem to think that timeless Christian references are enough.

There seems to be a hankering after an impossible ideal — pure theology. While the idealist pursuit is still in evidence there is no chance of overcoming perhaps the most dangerous of past theological errors: theological absolutism. Theology believes itself compelled to say the last word, to have the complete answer to every question, with the other sciences reduced to the level of "handmaids".

If theology is ever to discover its true historicity, the loss of this absolutist pretension would seem to be an absolute precondition. Discovering its true historicity simply means that it too is a provisional science, like the others, in the conditions of the time and place in which it operates. This is not pushing relativism to extremes, since a serious understanding of the primordial nature of the *locus theologicus* offered by the ambiguity of experience at the present time (the source of understanding of what is provisional on one hand, but the means of incarnation on the other) in no way implies losing sight of trans-historic references — both those from Christianity's past and those devolving from the eschatological perspective of the "kingdom of God". What is implied, though, is that these references should not be used in an a-historical manner, dragged down from an abstract heaven in which truth is consistent only with itself, without regard for the historical processes through which man became a hearer of the word.

Apart from the fundamental revision of its most basic categories required by this recognition of theology's provisional nature (revelation, the word of God, and so on), it will also undergo a profound shift of emphasis. This provisional and humble theology will not be primarily interested in the task of establishing an abstract truth in a non-temporal sense, but will seek to set truth in time as an historic, and therefore effective, force. Its main interest will be truth made love, truth-practice, "making true". The central preoccupation of the theologian who has accepted the provisional nature of his "making theology" will no longer be the interpretation of the world, but its transformation.

Once it is accepted as provisional, theology can have no more pretensions to being "pure", and the way is open for a humble dialogue with the human and social sciences. Once the ideological function, in the pejorative sense of idealizing everything, has gone, then it becomes possible to use ideology as an instrument for the transformation of the world.

What is original and specific in Judaeo-Christianity is its insistence on the need to historicize the experience of faith. The paradoxical result of this originality is the need to abandon any sort of "complete specification" of the historical Christian process. If what is specific in Christianity is making man take on the full implications of his historical worldliness, this specific character of Christianity also excludes any specifically Christian advance definition of historical process in the world. Just as God becomes incarnate in what is not God, to the point where incarnation in "the other" becomes a specific mark of God, so the Christian is called to a *kenosis* or self-emptying consubtantial with his faith: that which is specific to his faith is not hanging greedily on to what is "its own", but rather losing itself in "the other", in the historical embodiment of his faith in the world. Basically, it is the same paradox as that of the material identity between love of God and love of "not-God" — the "other than God" who is our neighbour.

Theology has to go through the same paradox: of being itself only through not being itself. That means that the criteria for "good theology" cannot be strictly theological, just as the criteria for love of God are not found in the "divine order", but in effective love of our neighbour, in the "not divine" order. If what is "theological" in love of one's neighbour is seeing God in that neighbour, then what is theological in theological reflection on historical practice is its dimension of faith. But if the divine can only be found through the human, it then becomes entirely logical that a Christian theology will only find its truly theological character in its examination of the human process of history.

Any theology that does not seek its final and definitive theologicity in history will have abdicated in advance from the possibility of discussing the ultimate manifestation of love.

There is of course a radically mysterious dimension to love made history, which cannot be scientifically quantified or qualified, but only alluded to in art and poetry and the symbolism of the mystics. But that is no excuse for theology to stay light years away from the overall reality of the historical practice of love, because many of its components can be named and analyzed, even if the whole eludes definition.

If theology fails to speak the language of love embodied in historical fact, it is bound to fall back on idealism and ideology. Christ on the cross is a historical and political demonstration of love in action; in failing to point that out, theology has in fact done no more than invent ideological interpretations of the historical importance of this complete surrender of self. And ideology has always been the road to removal from the sphere of history.

2. *Social setting means strategy and tactics*

The need to interpret the original data of theological sources by way of the data of the secular sciences is only one of the methodological consequences for this provisional and historical theology. In Latin America we are now very decidedly at the point where the incorporation in their own right of the secular sciences, particularly the social sciences, in theological thinking, is seen to be a basic requirement. That, in a way, is the originality of Latin American theology. But it is not the end of the matter: we have gone a step or two further, and gained a clear understanding of the ethical and political decision implicit in the choice of a sociological instrument of analysis; furthermore, we have not rejected the ideological step entailed in choosing a particular ethical or political system. And when I say "we", I am not talking of a few committed individuals. This is now the basic element of theological thinking in the theology of liberation.

This is what is happening: in Latin America we are beginning to reflect on the Christian faith, focusing more and more definitely on its overall, actual historical configuration. The theology that is emerging is consciously trying to be part of historical practice as well as critical reflection on it; its social viewpoint is determinedly realist, rejecting the idealism still characteristic of the theology of the affluent societies. We are beginning to draw the consequences from the fact that Christian faith is inseparable from a social, economic and political (historical) process. We are equally beginning to realize the consequences of the fact that the true stature of love can only be grasped through its historical embodiments; and here general "Christian" criteria are powerless and negatively ideological.

Any talk of the historical implications of Christian commitment has to come down to the level of the strategy and tactics of the fight for liberation. Theology, even as a "science", must be a "rebel science", and a committed one; it must take sides and place itself at the service of groups recognized as being in the van in the process of liberation, just as the social sciences are doing.

As I see it, the novelty of this form of theology consists in its open use of ideology as a weapon in the struggle for the transformation of the New World, and at the same time its consciousness of the precarious nature of its word.

Once set on this path, the Latin American theologian is still going to find himself alone, almost devoid of links with the Christian reference-points of the past, both on the level of essential doctrine, and on that of the historical forms taken by the institution charged with mediating that doctrine in history. He is a conscious "apostate" from the idealisms of the past and those that are arising again today. Like any apostate rebelling iconoclastically against the idols of the past, he finds it difficult — for linguistic and other reasons — to make his brothers understand that he is not just an iconoclast but an opener of new horizons on the use of the name of God.

NOTES

[1] Held at Buenos Aires in June 1971, and Bogotá in July 1971.
[2] G. Gutiérrez, *A Theology of Liberation, op. cit.*; P. Richard, "La negación de lo 'cristiano' como afirmación de la fe", in *Cuadernos de la Realidad Nacional* (Santiago de Chile, April 1972), pp. 144-53.
[3] O. Fals Borda, *Ciencia propia y colonialismo intelectual* (Mexico, 1970), p. 34. The book is a very clear account, with a good bibliography, of the revolution that has taken place in the social sciences in Latin America.
[4] This is the translation of the title of a book by M. Kaplan, *La ciencia política latinoamericana en la encrucijada* (Santiago de Chile, 1970).
[5] The phrases are from O. Fals Borda, *op. cit.*; O. Varansky, in his *Ciencia, política y cientificismo* (Buenos Aires, 1969), also speaks of the need for a "guerrilla science".

IV The Christian contribution to liberation in Latin America

IV The Christian contribution to liberation in Latin America

PERHAPS the first important contribution Christians can make to the process of liberation is not to add to the process of diluting the revolutionary implications that circumstances have dictated it should contain.

I do not propose to deal with the Christian contribution in a universal or idealist fashion; what is of concern is not what this contribution *should* be, but what it *is* and *can be* in the present circumstances. I shall concentrate on real events and possible events, not on what we might like to see happening ideally.

I. What is meant by the process of liberation

Once more, I have to begin with a reminder that commitment to the process of liberation in Latin America means starting from a particular analysis of our situation as oppressed peoples; that opting for a particular social analysis is not a neutral step. It involves the necessary choice of an ethical and political stance; there is no such thing as an uninvolved social science, and to pretend that there is is itself to adopt a reactionary ideological position. This fact has already become central to discussions of methodology on the level of the social sciences. There is probably no more obvious example of a committed science anywhere today than sociology in Latin America, which has taken the decisive step of making "dependence" the central theme of its investigations into the real situation in Latin America. This situation of dependence is the basic starting-point for the process of liberation. On the theological level an analysis of dependence has produced the language of the theology of liberation. That is not a natural development from post-conciliar church reform, but a decisive break with the earlier language of development and all that it signified on the sociological, political and other levels.

Talking of liberation implies taking a new analytical stance with regard to the situation of our countries, a basically new conception of the phenomenon of under-development, and, consequently, a new point of departure from which to map out the political and economic ways out of this situation. The conclusions drawn are inevitably revolutionary, and the language of liberation is the language that articulates them. This relates it directly to the new analysis of under-development. It springs *pari passu* from the accumulated frustrations produced by "development" models and expresses our rejection of them.

The theory of dependence springs from the crisis of the theory of development. Rather than complementing it, it represents its total rejection, seeing under-development not as a backward state preceding developed capitalism, but as a direct consequence of it, a special and engineered form of development: dependent capitalism. The fact that dependence has been a situation constant throughout our history, and productive of it, means that it can become a scientific category to explain our history: under-development as a form of dependence.

Dependence is not simply an "external factor" affecting international relations; it is a situation that has moulded the internal structures of our countries. Dependence can be seen as part of the world-wide framework of imperialism, but it has a reality of its own. One has not only to broaden one's concept of imperialism, but to reformulate it in some essential aspects.

The process of liberation comes to mean the new revolutionary direction the countries of Latin America must take if they are to find a real way out of their situation as dependants. The newness of this direction consists in its total break with the ways sought through development in its various guises, including those masquerading as "Third World roads" (state capitalism, revolutionary nationalism, and so on).

The option for a way "of liberation" has not yet been taken in the strategic and tactical details of how the struggle for liberation is to be carried out, such as, for example, whether one way can be taking power through the electoral process in order to radicalize the power structure later, as happened in Allende's Chile; or what the first steps in economic liberation have to be. The abstract option has to be translated into action according to the circumstances. There can be no real commitment to liberate one's country on the general level alone. Liberation, if it is to be an effective revolutionary way to the ending of dependence, has to include the working out of a strategy (which must involve choosing a particular political approach), and of the tactical steps for carrying out this strategy in the light of the most urgent needs.

In terms of political activity, this means not evading commitment on the burning struggle and tactical questions implicit in defining what one means by "party", "proletariat", "vanguard", "methods of action", and so on. Nevertheless, to talk in general terms of the process of liberation, provided that one takes account of the minimal elements implied by the anti-development option, in itself involves elements of social analysis and political approach, which enable us to establish basic demarcation-lines between the differing viewpoints of Christians and the rest of the population. Of course we have to beware of a vague commitment to liberation that shies away from involvement in the practical result.

II. The Christian approach to liberation

The major factor to be taken into account in the Latin American situation is the growing, clear and definite choice that *avant-garde* Christian groups are making in favour of commitment to liberation, on the basis of the sociological analysis already referred to and in full consciousness of the necessary implications. The situation in each country varies.

Perhaps one of the most significant new aspects is the

growing severity with which committed Christian groups are approaching the task of liberation. For them, general statements and proclamations are not enough; those who require a definite connexion between ideological and political thinking on liberating action, and reflection on faith as the historical embodiment of love, are far from unthinking activists. They remember too well past frustrations in this field, such as the rapid evaporation of the euphoria that followed the second Vatican council and the Medellín Conference, and the subsequent withdrawals into ecclesiastical reform.

1. The churches on a world scale

The ecclesiastical hierarchies of the various Christian denominations and the ecclesiastical bodies responsible for social questions (the Justice and Peace Commission and its equivalent on the World Council of Churches, various national institutes, and so on) have not yet assimilated the more prickly implications of the process of liberation, and show no signs of doing so in the immediate future.

Nevertheless, there have been some signs of progress in Christian social doctrine, even in official documents such as papal encyclicals and the declarations of the Beirut and Uppsala conferences, and in some more or less symbolic acts, such as the financing of liberation movements in Africa by the World Council of Churches, which have begun to show world opinion a swing on the part of the churches towards a revolutionary position. This impression is of course a significant break with the conservative image that the churches have presented up till now, and Christianity as a whole is viewed even by Marxists as a source of energy behind the process of changing the world.

Yet despite these auguries, the churches of the affluent societies are structurally incapable of becoming even more or less open "support areas" in the struggle for liberation in Latin America, except in the most general terms of drawing attention to international injustices, abandoning their naively anti-Communist stance, tolerating the progress made by certain Christian action groups, and so on. All these phenomena are signs of a certain loosening of the earlier rigid attitude toward explicit revolutionary ideals. Basically, however, the churches of the affluent world remain inward-looking, concerned in a bureaucratic way with internal ecclesiastical affairs — with a "social action" sector as it were tacked on to the main body. In theological terms one can ask whether they are actually remaining true to their own doctrine on the nature of the Church, which is to be an organ of service to mankind. The Church cannot find its *raison d'être* in itself, in the internal workings of its structures, because its vocation is one of radical service to the world. Without discounting the importance of the ecclesial aspect, with its centre in worship and the proclamation of the word, it would seem that what the churches themselves proclaim as their missionary nature should imply a far more decided shift to a stress on the "world" pole of their activities.

"Political non-intervention" is still one of the most explicitly cultivated charactersitics of the churches of the developed world. It is exported to the Third World. The classic ideological and pseudo-theological grounds for this attitude — the Church's special mission, the autonomy of the temporal sphere, and so forth — constantly reappear under new guises, with new theological pretexts — secularization theology, for one. These churches still do not seem to have grasped the political significance of their so-called non-political stance. Even where there are some signs of a theoretical change of heart, their superstructure of ethics, doctrine and legalism lags a long way behind taking any practical steps to put it into effect.

The progressive elements in exegesis and theology in the affluent world, with a few exceptions, concentrate on matters of only peripheral relevance to really major world problems. It would, as I have said, be virtually impossible to get an international theological congress to agree on a concept like "under-development as a form of dependence". The sometimes aggressive manner in which Latin American theologians now reject even the progressive contributions of the developed world is quite understandable. Without disparaging the undoubted contribution that European and North American theology has made to the development of thinking in other areas, it cannot as a whole be described as a theology sensitive to the urgent demands of history or as one that has contributed to sensibilizing the process of history. In many cases it has demonstrated a cynical insensitivity to the plight of the thirty million who die of starvation and malnutrition each year, as well as to the clamour for liberation arising from the oppressed.

As far as world opinion is concerned, the chief spokesmen for Christianity are still the Christians of the developed world. They are "the Christian world". "Baptized" Latin America is the exception in the Third World. This is perhaps a major sociological factor in the special vocation of the Church in Latin America, and one that will lead to a growing alienation from the Christians of the developed world if they continue on their present course. Geography is coming to be an essential ingredient of Christian witness.

2. The churches of Latin America: official and popular

If dependence is the situation that decides the condition of our countries, not as some simple external factor but as the historical determinant of the internal components of our present reality, then this interpretative key is also basic to our understanding of the situation of Latin American Christianity. It is a dependent Christianity. That is a simplification, but it should be borne in mind to avoid falling into inconsistencies and euphoric expectations of rapid and radical change in the structures of Latin American Christianity, particularly at the level of ecclesiastical hierarchies and the baptized masses. Although there are signs of initial breaks in certain aspects of this dependence, the mechanics of dependence remain powerful at infra- and super-structural levels.

Not only is no explicit change in the present direction of commitment to the process of liberation discernible at either hierarchy or mass level, but there is no sign of such a thing happening in the near future. It cannot therefore be relied upon as a possibility in any strategy of liberation. What is evident is a general, verbal drawing near to the theme of liberation, evident even in documents emanating from official sources. But that cannot be taken as implying even a theoretical understanding of the historical implications of the process of liberation, let alone any effective commitment that will result in action. On these levels, in other words, one cannot say there is a definite rejection of development models and a clear new historical consciousness opposed to the *status quo*.

Nevertheless, the churches in Latin America are changing, at the official level, and even overall, by comparison with those of the developed world. The language may still be vague, but it is different, and so are the priorities. A language of vague denouncement of injustice, that would be totally impotent in other circumstances, may still have some power in Latin America; in the same way, small groups can wield an influence out of proportion to their numbers. Prophetic minorities often come to exert a surprising influence at the level of decision-making, particularly when they meet and issue declarations.

The churches in Latin America today often seem to be leap-frogging over each other in their desire to make verbal advances. This creates the ambiguous phenomenon of a sort of *kenosis* leading to inevitable re-thinking but at the same time to a new set of reference-points from which those who are determined to go forward can start. Perhaps the greatest novelty, and the one of most political significance, is the impression of decided advance made on public opinion, which has so frightened some governments. The Right is more and more coming to the conclusion that it cannot count on the support of the Church, whereas the Left is beginning to regard it as a potential ally.

It may be no exaggeration to say that this impression — and it is still more impression than reality — of a broadening of the base of support for liberation on the part of the churches, is in fact becoming a real beachhead, acting as a sort of self-fulfilling prophecy. The Medellín documents are perhaps the clearest example of this process in action: issued with the highest official credentials, they in fact propose measures beyond the capabilities of the bishops; the bishops therefore cannot adopt them, but they become a rallying-point for the *avant-garde*, which in turn prods the consciences of the hierarchies and those Christians who have not yet made up their minds, who therefore begin to give at least verbal support. The impression is then created of an at least half-formed alliance between the official and *avant-garde* Church.

But there are still structural blockages, brought about by

an ethics and a theology conditioned by a "middle-class" background (ideologically the churches were formed by the upper and middle strata of society), and by strong outside pressures brought to bear by the churches of the affluent world, whose domination is no less real, though more subtle and respectful in form. Some examples: the continued attempt to disavow prophetic groups operating outside official channels; the doctrine of unity at any price; the inability to face conflicts in society openly and name them; verbal insistence on the force of charity conceived without its historical dimension; or on the universal validity of some vague social teaching of the Church, without subjecting it to analysis in terms of locally valid strategy and tactics; and finally, since the process of shifting the option towards the historical process and its demands is still far from complete, a continual temptation to slide back into internal ecclesiastical concentration on purely pastoral reforms.

The greatest differences between Christians, therefore, are no longer those between pre-conciliar traditionalists and post-conciliar progressives (who are equally preoccupied almost exclusively with internal pastoral reforms and tend to be politically inactive). The real discrepancy is between those who, fed on North-Atlantic progressive theology, are concerned with internal church reform, and those who are motivated and committed by the prior challenges of the process of liberation. This discrepancy is taking on the dimensions of an abyss.

3. *Christians committed to liberation*

Who are they? On the basic strategical and tactical level, there are groups of all sorts, the best-known being those formed basically by priests and pastors and "ministerial communities" from the different churches. In the "Christian" socio-cultural subsoil of Latin American society, their impact has been the greatest. The polarizing power of Camilo Torres's action should be seen in this context. Typical groups are: Priests of the Third World, in Argentine; Golconda, in Columbia; the Young Church, in Chile. In Bolivia, one group, ISAL, has had a really astonishing impact. Its composition is original too: its constitution was drawn up by Protestants, but its membership is more than 90% Catholic; it has an unusually large secular membership, many of them confessed Marxists. For many, including priests and nuns, ISAL-Bolivia has become almost a new Church. This is not the place to examine its complexity and possible ambiguities of motivation; suffice to say that its political stance has placed it in the van of the struggle for liberation.

It should not be forgotten that if Christian participation in the struggle for liberation is now a "major event" — just as the theology of liberation is seen to be above all a critical reflection on the actions of those who participate in this major event — this is due primarily to the growing lay presence in the front ranks of the struggle. This is not the place for a detailed account of the methods used by each group in working out the tactics they will employ in their commitment; what is important is the tremendous impression made by the growing number of Christians active in movements of the new Left, in direct action groups, such as the Tupamaros and others, and national liberation fronts. One example was the case of Teoponte, in Bolivia, where (as I have described in a book withdrawn from circulation by the Bolivian police in 1971, and re-published in Caracas in 1972) the Christian participation in the guerrilla activity was a decisive factor in its outcome.

The distinctive elements that characterize the growing Christian option for the struggle for liberation would seem to be the following:

(*a*) The increasingly conscious acceptance of the sociological implications of a new concept of development, in the terms I have described earlier. The adoption of the language of liberation among Christian groups is closely connected with an appreciation of the mounting frustrations arising from the concept of development.

(*b*) Their anti-development stance is what commits them in the first instance to the concept of liberation. This has weighty consequences; firstly, because the churches at world level cannot keep up at this point, and secondly, because the political implications are quite definite in the context of different countries. In Bolivia, for example, it involved the rejection of the option offered by "revolutionary nationalism", and opposition both to the vagueness of the government of the day as well as to the imperialist charter proposed by the MNR (National Revolutionary Movement).

(*c*) On the political level, these groups see the need to express their views by unequivocal commitment. Their reflection on faith as the historical process of liberation has to operate on the level of strategy and tactics, as well as on that of ideas.

(*d*) Theologically, they effectively embody a shift of the basic reference-point of their faith, which is no longer a body of doctrine, or a form of worship (both of which remain important, but in a complementary role), but the territory occupied by the historical process of liberation. This evidently entails a fresh look at their manner of belonging to the Church and a revision of the central tenets of traditional theology. What emerges very clearly is that the prophetic element of Christianity — prophecy as word and action — acquires a greater importance for them than the institutional element.

(*e*) In general they realize that the traditional contributions of Christian social teaching — which has been discussed with growing freedom in Latin America in recent years — are wholly inadequate for acting on the more radical implications of faith as the practice of liberation. As a result, until a viable Christian body of thought can be elaborated, they inevitably turn to the analytical techniques of Marxism, often without taking account of the possible overall consequences.

(*f*) For many, the step beyond the euphoria of being "revolutionaries in theory", imposed by involvement in real action, has brought a full realization of the ambiguity, originality and isolation of their position seen in the context of world-wide Christianity. This brings a fresh seriousness to both their political and theological reflection and their actions.

(*g*) An increasingly significant element is the realization that their commitment to liberation means introducing the class struggle into the Church itself. They know they are not *with* other Christians, but rather *in open conflict with* the majority of them. But they also know there is no escaping this minority opposition role, because they have to range themselves on the side of the exploited. Hence the theme of conflict in history and in present-day reality has become so central to the theology of revolution. They find themselves obliged to denounce the ideology of a false unity-without-conflict in the Church, which is a major point of difference between them and others in viewing the whole historical existence of the Church. They can no longer accept that eucharistic conditions can automatically obtain in a Church that includes oppressors and oppressed. An element of tension and conflict is introduced at the centre of the life of faith. Its practical implications can easily be imagined.

III. The Christian contribution

1. Breaching the superstructure

There is a serious limitation to the Christian contribution to liberation which has been a source of frustration to many committed Christians. It need not be so in the Latin-American context.

If one analyzes the impact made to date by the presence of Christians in liberation movements, the area in which they have been most effective is that of the superstructure represented by traditional bourgeois values, in which they have opened a major breach. In that sense, Christian revolutionary action has already been most effective; for the traditional concept of the ideal Christian above all as a man of "peace", pacifically stationed within the existing order, quietly collaborating with the rules of the game of the *status quo*, has virtually become a thing of the past.

But is that the first objective of the revolutionary process? In Marxist terms, obviously not: the structural changes brought about by the process of liberation should be primarily on the level of the infrastructure — economic, social and political — but always at the grassroots level. Christian revolutionary aims are evidently in the same direction, but has their influence been appropriate so far?

It all depends on how one views historical effectiveness. There is a short term and a long term. Those who look only for the short term have to discount many actions as ineffective — guerrilla activity in Latin America to date would probably be the prime example. But, if we take a longer view of the revolutionary process, the opposite might be true: it is a long process, with many different steps to be taken, and apparent failures often come to be seen as having made a tremendously significant contribution to later successes.

Furthermore, strictly orthodox Marxism often seems incapable of appreciating the features peculiar to the Latin American situation. I do not want to undertake a cultural analysis here, as it would be inadequate unless integrated with the results of a structural dialectical analysis. It is essential to understand the "relative autonomy" of the elements that make up the superstructure of our society, because this is where many of the obstacles to change are to be found. If obstacles could be removed at that level, a significant contribution would be made to the revolutionary process. The obstacles to change at "superstructure" level, particularly those represented by *petit-bourgeois* values and the tendency to acquiesce in the passivity of the populace, undoubtedly owe much to pseudo-Christian traditions and values both in origin and maintenance. In this context, it is worth recalling what Engels wrote to Josef Bloch on the subject of false interpretation of Marx and himself by those who believed that Marxism had to concentrate exclusively on the proletariat: "According to the materialist view of history, the factor that determines history in the final instance is the production and reproduction of real life. Neither Marx nor I have ever said more than that. The economic situation is the base, but various elements of the superstructure that rises from it (the political forms of the class struggle and its consequences, the constitutions that the victorious class draws up once the battle is won, and juridical forms . . .) also exert their influence on the course of historical events and determine their shape — in some cases, more than any other factor".

From the Christian point of view, the fact that liberation in Latin America involves important changes in the superstructure has an added significance in regard to a basic point of faith: man is born of the gift of the Lord; he is created, as man, from outside. That may sound vague, but it has very definite implications, directly related to our faith in revelation. Man does not appear as a spontaneous product of structures, even though these are the necessary conditioning material of his "birth" as a new man. If the formative context of material structures is not joined by the loving process of call and response, the result is a simple product of the environment and not the new man. Hence the much-used Christian term "witness" still retains its full meaning at the heart of the liberation process. Nor should it be forgotten that the new revolutionary ethic that was Che Guevara's constant dream was based on this concept — a concept that makes use of most specific channels for the efficacy of love in its transformation of history.

If, however, the Christian contribution to the revolution has so far been most effective in removing obstacles at superstructure level, that does mean that Christians cannot yet claim to be the "revolutionary vanguard" pure and simple, because they are in fact acting as auxiliaries to the vanguard and no more. They must accept this as their position. Whilst this is conducive to humility, it should not lead them to belittle their own efforts, but to deepen their effective commitment still further. The Christian guerrillas of Teoponte were radical to the end in their actions, but their chief effect was to breach the superstructure of that Bolivia characterized by traditions and native religions, with its superficial "Christian" overlay, and tremendously retarded by elements of "religiosity" in the superstructure of its society.

2. Revolution in the infrastructure

Those who take the plunge of a real option for the process of liberation have to recognize, on the basis of their sociological analysis, that changes in the infrastructure of our countries must be at the root of any true revolution. But what genuine Christian contribution can be made to this process?

First of all, Christians have to be open in declaring their revolutionary objectives. An open challenge to imperialism, from within and without, is not merely a revolutionary slogan, but the basis on which the changes to come have to be made on the infrastructure level. Not only can there be no revolution without revolutionary theory — just as, conversely, there can be no revolutionary theory without action, because the theory has to be a theory of action — but there can be no true revolutionary theory without working out a historical project. Revolutionary theory is more than the simple tactical elaboration of a method of fighting; it is that, but more too: it has to include plans for the objectives of liberation in the form of a historical project. This can be a long business. In the Latin American context, the political situation and the urgency of the struggle have tended to lead left-wing groups to reduce to a minimum their statement of a clear historical project. Here Christians have a real contribution to make, and not merely on the level of repeating fragmentary political platforms for immediate political consumption. There is in fact already a growing Christian presence among the true theorists of the aims and methods of the process of liberation.

The question of who forms the revolutionary vanguard is intimately linked to that of the infrastructural changes needed. The oppressed and the exploited, those who have a vital interest in the outcome of revolution, become the revolutionary vanguard when the revolution is really made for them and by them. Those who are directly concerned in the changes to come are really called to form the van of the revolution in the true sense of the term. This again is a many-sided question, and one which Christians have tended to approach with a certain lack of historical realism, dreaming of a revolution inspired by pure love, while the Marxists recognize that it will be carried out by those who have a direct interest in its success. Historically incarnate love is in no sense removed from interests, provided "interests" is not understood in the bourgeois, individualist sense. The clear definition and realization of the interests of the oppressed is the historical embodiment of love. Christians will more easily become authentic revolutionaries the more they identify their way of life with that of the exploited. This evidently should not be taken as meaning that those Christians of middle-class extraction, who are disinterestedly fighting for the interests of those who stand to benefit from the revolution, and against their own interests, cannot be true revolutionaries. Their kenotic or self-emptying presence can even have a humanizing influence on the revolutionary process, but this must not be idealized as an act of idyllic, abstract and *petit-bourgeois*-style love.

The process of liberation aims at being an anti-imperialist (and on the national level, anti-oligarchic) and at the same time an anti-technocratic revolution. The latter aspect is clear from its anti-development stance. The double perspective distinguishes it from earlier revolutionary models. If the liberation we are seeking aims not only at an adequate supply of goods for all, but at active human participation at all levels, it opens up a whole range of questions and problems, all of which coincide with the deepest Christian concerns for the welfare of man.

3. How effective?

Our final consideration is the vexed question of a "specifically Christian" contribution to liberation. I believe this has usually been presented in a false, pretentious and triumphalist manner which assumes that Christians must know more than non-believers about the true human character of liberation. But instead of worrying about their "specific contribution", surely what Christians in growing numbers ought to do is to make a real contribution to the process as they find it? Constantly to insist on the original dynamism of the social teaching of the churches, and blithely to pass over the terrible sociological fact of the massive reactionary presence of "Christianity" in practice, merely transforms what is best in Christianity — its effective possibility of being a real humanizing influence — into trivial ideology.

In the present sociological situation of world-scale Christianity as well as in Latin America, neither the structures of the Church nor the theology in vogue offer any natural resources for a specifically Christian contribution to liberation. Nowhere is there evident, even on the theoretical level, a Christian understanding of man so incarnate in our historical reality that it alone can provide the definite imperatives for a more complete work of humanization.

But this does not exhaust the question of the "specific" contribution Christians can make. That is still a valid question and one that is vital to those of us who believe in embodying the love that springs from the sources of our faith. But we have to learn humility again; we do not know it all so well. Nor are we the only ones concerned with the truly loving dimension of the problem of living together as human beings. The general direction in which we have to look for a specifically Christian contribution seems clear enough: it is in what is specifically and fully human, in the line of fidelity to all that is involved materially in loving one's neighbour. But theoretical insistence is not enough: we have an overall vision of the purpose of man to urge us to action. A truly historical reading of the Bible, particularly of the message of Christ, leads to a whole series of radical questions to which Marxism has not paid sufficient attention, of which perhaps the most significant is the Christian affirmation of victory over death, that final alienation to which Marxism can find no satisfactory answer.

Tackling this infidelity to history, the aspect that emerges as most significant is not the belief in "something after death" (which can easily become selfish), but this: The God who raised Jesus from the dead is not a God of the dead but also of the living. Since life is God's "medium", he also wants it to be man's sphere above all else. Once this is understood in an historical and trans-historical sense, in terms of a Christian eschatology whose questions about ultimate meaning can only be grasped through historical and immediate questions, we come to the marrow of the loving mystery of what it means to risk one's life for one's fellow men. Marxism asks all revolutionaries to be prepared to do this, but I do not believe it can really answer the question of the human sense of laying down one's life for others — so deeply relevant to revolutionary practice — nor that it has really tried to see the importance of the problem.

I believe that the Christian formula "love = death-life", kept on a historical and existential plane, can become the key to the series of radical conundrums that impose themselves daily on those who live entirely for others. Perhaps this is the best way to understand the specifically Christian contribution to liberation.

Conclusion

In conclusion I must stress the urgent need of specific action in Christian witness. It must reflect a commitment made in specific circumstances and having a specific outcome. Reflection on the challenges our faith presents us with in history is a precious necessity. But there is no sense in discussing these matters in the abstract unless discussion leads to the one thing that counts: our effective commitment to the liberation of the oppressed.

Liberation

The time is coming
Latin America my land
When our frontiers will be borders of flowers
And our guns weapons of wood
You can see the dawn rising
The light in our darkness
You can hear the future
As our people sing

Latin America my land
Young woman rising from sleep
Who gave you your beauty?
And who your bitterness?

If death takes me
It is not for ever
I shall live in my songs
For you I shall live for ever
Forward the banners go
Forward for freedom
Sing with me
For our freedom is here

How good the days smell
The sweet air is ripe
And all the guitars sing
for the morning
I believe in a life to come
That men call justice
When all whom I love
Will smile for ever

That time is coming
Latin America my land

FELIX LUNA